I0029571

Workforce Development in Emerging Economies

DIRECTIONS IN DEVELOPMENT
Human Development

Workforce Development in Emerging Economies

Comparative Perspectives on Institutions, Praxis, and Policies

Jee-Peng Tan, Kiong Hock Lee, Ryan Flynn, Viviana V. Roseth, and Yoo-Jeung Joy Nam

WORLD BANK GROUP

© 2016 International Bank for Reconstruction and Development / The World Bank
1818 H Street NW, Washington, DC 20433
Telephone: 202-473-1000; Internet: www.worldbank.org

Some rights reserved

1 2 3 4 19 18 17 16

This work is a product of the staff of The World Bank with external contributions. The findings, interpretations, and conclusions expressed in this work do not necessarily reflect the views of The World Bank, its
Board of Executive Directors, or the governments they represent. The World Bank does not guarantee the
accuracy of the data included in this work. The boundaries, colors, denominations, and other information
shown on any map in this work do not imply any judgment on the part of The World Bank concerning the
legal status of any territory or the endorsement or acceptance of such boundaries.

Nothing herein shall constitute or be considered to be a limitation upon or waiver of the privileges and
immunities of The World Bank, all of which are specifically reserved.

Rights and Permissions

This work is available under the Creative Commons Attribution 3.0 IGO license (CC BY 3.0 IGO) http://
creativecommons.org/licenses/by/3.0/igo. Under the Creative Commons Attribution license, you are free to
copy, distribute, transmit, and adapt this work, including for commercial purposes, under the following
conditions:

Attribution—Please cite the work as follows: Tan, Jee-Peng, Kiong Hock Lee, Ryan Flynn, Viviana V. Roseth,
    and Yoo-Jeung Joy Nam. 2016. *Workforce Development in Emerging Economies: Comparative Perspectives
    on Institutions, Praxis, and Policies.* Directions in Development. Washington, DC: World Bank.
    doi:10.1596/978-1-4648-0850-0. License: Creative Commons Attribution CC BY 3.0 IGO

Translations—If you create a translation of this work, please add the following disclaimer along with the
    attribution: *This translation was not created by The World Bank and should not be considered an official
    World Bank translation. The World Bank shall not be liable for any content or error in this translation.*

Adaptations—If you create an adaptation of this work, please add the following disclaimer along with the
    attribution: *This is an adaptation of an original work by The World Bank. Views and opinions expressed in
    the adaptation are the sole responsibility of the author or authors of the adaptation and are not endorsed by
    The World Bank.*

Third-party content—The World Bank does not necessarily own each component of the content
    contained within the work. The World Bank therefore does not warrant that the use of any third-
    party–owned individual component or part contained in the work will not infringe on the rights of
    those third parties. The risk of claims resulting from such infringement rests solely with you. If you
    wish to reuse a component of the work, it is your responsibility to determine whether permission is
    needed for that reuse and to obtain permission from the copyright owner. Examples of components
    can include, but are not limited to, tables, figures, or images.

All queries on rights and licenses should be addressed to the Publishing and Knowledge Division, The
World Bank, 1818 H Street NW, Washington, DC 20433, USA; fax: 202-522-2625; e-mail: pubrights
@worldbank.org.

ISBN (paper): 978-1-4648-0850-0
ISBN (electronic): 978-1-4648-0851-7
DOI: 10.1596/978-1-4648-0850-0

Cover photo: Darryl Estrine/Getty Images
Cover design: Debra Naylor, Naylor Design, Inc.

Library of Congress Cataloging-in-Publication Data has been requested.

Contents

Acknowledgments   *ix*
About the Authors   *xi*
Executive Summary   *xiii*
Abbreviations   *xvii*

Chapter 1   **Introduction**   1
              Notes   2
              References   2

Chapter 2   **Education and Skills for Growth in Emerging Economies**   5
              Pattern of Enrollments   5
              Cognitive, Technical, and Social-Emotional Skills   6
              Equipping the Workforce with Job-Relevant Skills   10
              Building Job-Relevant Skills through Preemployment
                 Training   10
              Building Job-Relevant Skills through Workplace Training   14
              Job-Relevant Skills for the Informal Economy   19
              Notes   22
              References   23

Chapter 3   **A Framework and Tool for Dialogue on Workforce
              Development**   31
              The SABER-WfD Conceptual Framework   32
              Features of the SABER-WfD Tool   34
              Notes   37
              References   38

Chapter 4   **Data and Highlights from the Application of the
              SABER-WfD Tool**   39
              Data Collection, Validation, and Analysis   39
              Pattern in Dimension-Level Scores across Countries   42
              Scores of Countries with Multiyear Data   44
              Selected Comparisons of Country Experiences over Time   46
              Notes   48
              References   49

Chapter 5   Underpinnings of the Dimension-Level
              SABER-WfD Scores   **51**
              Distribution of Countries by Dimension-Level Scores   51
              Strategic Framework and Its Underpinnings   53
              System Oversight and Its Underpinnings   57
              Service Delivery and Its Underpinnings   64
              Summary of Key Highlights for the 22 Countries   70
              Notes   71
              Reference   72

Chapter 6   **SABER-WfD and the Agenda for Systems Development**   **73**
              Broadening the Dialogue   74
              Integrating WfD into Strategies for Economic
                  Transformation   75
              Nurturing WfD Systems toward Maturity   78
              Building Capacity for Sustained Reform   80
              Notes   82
              References   84

Appendix A   **Market and Government Roles in Workforce
              Development**   **89**
              Notes   95
              References   96

Boxes

2.1   The Importance and Broadening of Social-Emotional Skills   9
2.2   The World Bank's STEP Conceptual Framework on Skills   11
2.3   Job-Relevant Soft Skills in Vocational Education and Training
           Programs   12
2.4   Evidence on Workplace Training and Productivity   16
2.5   Benin's Dual Apprenticeship System   21
4.1   Crowdsourcing SABER-WfD Data   40
6.1   Industrial Policy and Workforce Skills   76

Figures

2.1   Gross Enrollment Ratios by Education Level and Country
           Income Group, 1980–2010   6
2.2   Percentage Distribution of Students by Functional Numeracy,
           Selected Countries   8
B2.1   Five Key Policy Areas on Skills for Employment and
           Productivity   11

2.3   VET Enrollment Share by Level of Education and
         Country Group, 2000 and 2010   13
2.4   Per Student Public Spending on VET and Academic Programs at
         the Upper-Secondary Level, Selected Countries, circa 2009   14
2.5   Example of Flexible Pathways for Building Job-Relevant Skills
         through Links between VET and Tertiary Education   15
3.1   SABER-WfD's Conceptual Framework for Dialogue on
         Workforce Development   32
3.2   Three Functional Dimensions of Decision Making in the
         SABER-WfD Framework   34
3.3   Functional Dimensions and Major Topics in the
         SABER-WfD Tool   36
B4.1.1   Collecting SABER-WfD Data through Crowdsourcing   41
4.1   SABER-WfD Scoring Rubrics   42
4.2   Relation between Dimension-Level SABER-WfD Scores
         and GDP per capita, circa 2012   43
4.3   Dimension-Level SABER-WfD Scores in Five Countries,
         1970–circa 2010   45
5.1   Navigating the Presentation of the SABER-WfD
         Scores and Their Underpinnings   52
5.2   Distribution of Dimension-Level Scores   52
5.3   Strategic Framework and Its Underpinnings   53
5.4   Strategic Direction and the Underlying Drivers   54
5.5   Strategic Partnership and the Underlying Drivers   55
5.6   Strategic Coordination and the Underlying Drivers   56
5.7   System Oversight and Its Underpinnings   58
5.8   Funding Policy and the Underlying Drivers   59
5.9   Quality Assurance and the Underlying Drivers   61
5.10   Learning Pathways and the Underlying Drivers   63
5.11   Service Delivery and Its Underpinnings   65
5.12   Diversity and Excellence and the Underlying Drivers   66
5.13   Relevance of Public Provision and the Underlying Drivers   67
5.14   System Management and the Underlying Drivers   69
5.15   Highlights of SABER-WfD Findings for 22 Countries   71
A.1   Relationship between Standardized Scores and GDP
         Per Capita, by Dimension   93

Table
A.1   Detailed Summary of the SABER-WfD Findings for 22 Countries   94

Acknowledgments

This report is a product of the World Bank's initiative on Systems Approach for Better Education Results (SABER)—currently hosted in the Education Global Practice—which drives the institution's strategy for implementing its 10-year education plan issued in 2010. The report addresses workforce development challenges, one of several policy arenas considered in the SABER initiative. Using an analytical framework created under the initiative, it offers insights distilled from data for nearly 30 countries, including time-series information for some of them; and from country-specific analyses, which may be found at the SABER website at http://saber.worldbank.org/index.cfm.

The authors are grateful to those who provided input and guidance in the initial stages of this work when the analytical framework was being developed. They include: David Ablett, Hernan Araneda, David Ashton, Michael Axmann, Dan Baffour-Awuah, Sukdeep Brar, Renato Caporali, Birger Fredriksen, Kenneth King, Song Seng Law, Young-Hyun Lee, Peliwe Lolwana, Fook Low Wong, Robert McGough, John Middleton, Peter Moock, Gordon Nixon, Charlene Nunley, Juan Prawda, Michelle Riboud, Bianca Rohrbach, Shashi Shrivastava, Phillip Toner, Arvil Van Adams, Dan Vogler, and Saint William. Subsequent contributions from Richard Johanson are also much appreciated.

The authors thank those who piloted the first application of the SABER–Workforce Development instrument for data collection and analysis in five countries. They include: Cecilia Zanetta (Chile), Susan Leigh-Doyle (Ireland), Hye Won Ko and Yoon Hee Park (the Republic of Korea), Arwen Raddon (Singapore), and Jutta Franz (Uganda).

The authors acknowledge the critical role of World Bank staff who supported SABER–Workforce Development assessments around the world and facilitated the collection of the data that constitute the basis for the cross-country analysis presented here. They are: Meskerem Mulatu (Armenia and Georgia), Dandan Chen (Armenia, Georgia, and Timor-Leste), Plamen Danchev (Bulgaria), Omar Arias (Bulgaria), Amira Kazen (the Arab Republic of Egypt and Jordan), Angela Demas (Grenada and Saint Lucia), Harriet Nannyonjo (Grenada and St. Lucia), Laura Gregory (Iraq), Lianqin Wang (Iraq), Lars Sondergaard (Lao People's Democratic Republic), Bojana Naceva (the former Yugoslav Republic of Macedonia), Indhira Santos (FYR Macedonia), Ximena del Carpio (Malaysia), Anna Olefir (Moldova and Ukraine), Johannes Koettl (Moldova and Ukraine),

Kamel Braham (Morocco and Tunisia), Stephen Close (the Solomon Islands), Halil Dundar (Sri Lanka), Yevgeniya Savchenko (Sri Lanka), Sachiko Kataoka (Tajikistan), Jeffrey Waite (Tunisia), Simon Thacker (Tunisia), Ahmet Levent Yener (Turkey), Cristian Bodewig (Vietnam), Emanuela di Gropello (Vietnam), Stefanie Brodmann (West Bank and Gaza), and Tomomi Miyajima (the Republic of Yemen). The authors are grateful to the principal investigators and government counterparts in each country whose efforts ensured that the data are complete, are appropriately interpreted, and are consistent with the requirements for cross-country comparability.

The authors appreciate the guidance and suggestions of Omar Arias, Christian Bodewig, and Xiaoyan Liang, World Bank peer reviewers for this document. Errors of fact or interpretation are solely the authors' responsibility and should not be attributed to the World Bank, the governments of the countries included in this report, or researchers and others involved in country-specific data collection and report preparation. The authors' affiliations are as follows: Jee-Peng Tan initiated the report as leader of the SABER-WfD work program prior to her retirement from the World Bank in 2013. Kiong Hock Lee, Ryan Flynn, and Yoo-Jeung Joy Nam were World Bank consultants to the SABER-WfD work program. Viviana V. Roseth is a consultant on the Education Global Practice's Skills Team. The authors value the support for this work from Alexandria Valerio, global lead of the Skills Global Solutions Group and head of the SABER-WfD team, and from Luis Benveniste and other managers in the Education Global Practice with oversight responsibility for the SABER initiative.

Last, the authors are most grateful for the generous financial support from the government of the United Kingdom through UK Aid, the government of Korea through the Korean Trust Fund, and the government of Australia through its Department of Foreign Affairs and Trade.

About the Authors

Jee-Peng Tan is a freelance consultant with expertise in education policy in emerging economies. During her 32-year career at the World Bank, she led numerous initiatives to advance the organization's work on education around the globe, including debt relief for the social sectors, the Education for All Fast Track Initiative, and high-level dialogue between African and Asian policy makers on education and economic development strategies. At her last post before retirement, as adviser in the World Bank's Human Development Network, she led the Systems Approach for Better Education Results (SABER)–Workforce Development initiative, creating the analytical tools and methodology and overseeing their implementation in nearly 30 countries. Since her retirement, Tan has taught at the National University of Singapore, and continues to serve as lead consultant to a number of World Bank teams on education policy and strategy.

Kiong Hock Lee contributed to the development of the SABER–Workforce Development tool in his capacity as senior World Bank consultant to the team. He began his career in commercial banking in Malaysia before joining the Faculty of Economics and Administration, University of Malaya, where, in his capacity as lecturer, professor, and chairman of the Division of Analytical Economics, he taught courses on the economics of education and on labor and personnel economics. He has served as a consultant to the Economic Planning Unit, Prime Minister's Department, Malaysia; the Association of Southeast Asian Nations (ASEAN) Secretariat, the Asian Development Bank, the International Labour Organization, and the United Nations Development Programme (UNDP) on human resource development and labor market information systems. He has led and conducted reverse tracer studies on skills training, and is the coeditor of a three-volume longitudinal tracer study on the transition from school to work in Malaysia.

Ryan Flynn is a workforce and skills consultant in the World Bank's Sub-Saharan Africa Region, where he is coordinating the development of a results-based lending program to improve the skills pipeline for key industries in Tanzania. He served previously as a research analyst within the Education Global Practice. In this capacity, he worked on developing analytical tools and methodologies under the SABER workforce development systems benchmarking program.

He subsequently comanaged its implementation in more than 30 countries, has developed a variety of products for dissemination of findings, and led dialogue on results with policy makers and business leaders in Africa, Asia, and the Pacific. He has worked in the nonprofit sector on trade policy and as an educator, and is a recipient of a Fulbright-Hayes award for study of language pedagogy in Beijing, China.

Viviana V. Roseth is a consultant on skills and workforce development at the World Bank Group's Education Global Practice. In her work on the SABER initiative, she has engaged with more than 15 country teams across the globe to assess workforce development systems, identify priorities for reform, and provide technical assistance on interagency coordination and on training provider management. In her work on the Skills toward Employability and Productivity (STEP) Skills Measurement, she has analyzed household surveys from 12 countries and produced diverse publications on educational attainment, cognitive, socioemotional and job-relevant skills, and labor market outcomes. Before joining the World Bank in 2012, Roseth worked with nongovernmental organizations in Latin America and the United States on entrepreneurship education, civics education and training, afterschool literacy programs for vulnerable youth, and university administration.

Yoo-Jeung Joy Nam is a consultant with the Education Global Practice of the World Bank Group. She has previously worked in the Education and Social Protection units of the World Bank, focusing on issues pertaining to workforce development. She has contributed to the SABER–Workforce Development and the Partnership for Skills in Applied Sciences, Engineering, and Technology (PASET) initiatives, as well as to the 2013 *World Development Report* on jobs. In her work with the SABER initiative, she has been involved in the development of the data collection instrument, data collection efforts in Korea, and the provision of technical assistance for participating countries. She is currently pursuing a PhD in education policy at Teachers College, Columbia University, and is also a graduate fellow at the National Center for Children and Families, where she contributes to policy-relevant research on early childhood education and development.

Executive Summary

Investing in skills has risen to the top of the policy agenda today in rich and poor countries alike. As a development partner of emerging economies, the World Bank participates actively in this arena, mobilizing a combination of its assets: development finance, research and analysis, global knowledge, technical assistance, and the convening power to facilitate policy dialogue, including through workshops and study visits. This book contributes to the catalogue of the World Bank's work. It focuses on workforce development (WfD) systems and presents novel systems-level data generated by the SABER-WfD analytical tool, which was created to implement the Bank's 10-year Education Sector Strategy launched in 2012. Hosted as one among several tools under the SABER (Systems Approach for Better Education Results) initiative, SABER-WfD shares the initiative's premise, namely that systems development is at the heart of the work required to improve education and training outcomes in the World Bank's partner countries. In particular, the SABER-WfD tool focuses on building job-relevant skills. It complements tools that address other major policy arenas identified in the Bank's Skills toward Employment and Productivity (STEP) framework: investing in early childhood development and in basic schooling; encouraging entrepreneurship and innovation; and facilitating labor market mobility and job matching.

A key challenge of building job-relevant skills is equipping individuals with the knowledge, know-how, and behaviors required to land and keep jobs in today's labor market. Several major trends are converging to make it a central focus of policies for WfD. In many emerging economies, decades-long expansion of basic education has created a veritable tsunami of youths with the paper credentials to aspire to further education and training or to a smooth transition to desirable jobs. Meanwhile, pervasive technological change is transforming the workplace in almost every country, increasing the need for continuous upgrading and updating of workforce skills for all workers, not just those entering the labor market for the first time. In emerging economies, a major preoccupation is the role of skills development for economic transformation, for enhancing the productivity of firms, and for addressing the skills needs of workers in the informal economy, which in many countries remains a dominant source of jobs and livelihoods.

Many strands of dialogue can and do take place in this complex policy terrain. The SABER-WfD tool unifies this multifaceted exchange around a common conceptual framework and shared terminology for WfD systems and their underlying institutions and praxis. At its core, the framework recognizes the existence of a basic tension between skills supply and demand in building job-relevant skills. To manage this tension productively in a dynamic context requires aligning the actions of multiple stakeholders, on both sides of the supply-demand equation.

To examine workforce development, the SABER-WfD tool focuses on three mechanisms for alignment: governance, finance, and information. It then examines the mechanisms at three functional levels or dimensions of decision making: (1) Strategic Framework, (2) System Oversight, and (3) Service Delivery. These dimensions correspond to actions under the purview of high-level officials and others with mandates above the sector ministries, authorities at the level of line ministries with responsibility for WfD (typically education, labor, youth, etc.), and those at the level of service provision.

Based on its conceptual framework, the SABER-WfD tool relies on a standardized data collection instrument and consistent protocols to gather data for comparative analysis across countries. The report presents the results for 27 countries and the West Bank and Gaza, five of them with aggregated time-series information. The qualitative data are scored, based on standard rules for placing each aspect of WfD institutions and praxis considered by the SABER-WfD tool, into one of four categories of performance, as follows:

Latent, signifying limited engagement,
Emerging, signifying some instances of good practice,
Established, signifying systemic good practice, and
Advanced, signifying good practice meeting global standards.

Among the main findings is that across countries, the scores for all three functional dimensions—Strategic Framework, System Oversight, and Service Delivery—rise with per capita gross domestic product (GDP). This pattern coheres with expectations that institutions and praxis would mature as wealth increases. But the scores for Strategic Framework generally dominate those for the other two functional dimensions; its lead is unchallenged in high-performing WfD systems, where no aspect is rated below Established. This position is no longer maintained in low-performing systems, where no part of the system rates above Emerging.

These patterns are consistent with trends over time in the five countries for which longitudinal data were available: Chile, Ireland, the Republic of Korea, Malaysia, and Singapore. The time-series results lead to these key findings:

• The score for Strategic Framework always tops the scores, at least by the time systems reach an Established level across dimensions.

- Although no score stagnates, raising any score does take time, often decades rather than years.
- The scores improve along diverse trajectories across countries, likely reflecting the influence of differences in broader economic context and the decisions taken by system leaders to cope with contextual factors.

Taken together, these cross country and time-series findings stress the importance of putting on a systems lens in policy dialogue about WfD. Such a lens brings into focus the disparate building blocks of WfD systems and their links to the broader economic and social policy context. It recognizes that what goes on within the education and training system, while important, is insufficient for framing the challenge of building job-relevant skills.

The more detailed country-level SABER-WfD findings identify lagging areas that could trigger discussions on priorities for policy reform, a process that has already occurred to varying degrees in these countries. The cross-country results also reveal common challenges in emerging economies that can help sharpen international dialogue on and support for strengthening WfD systems. Noteworthy among these results are the following:

- Under the Strategic Framework dimension, forming and sustaining strategic partnerships with employers poses more challenges than articulating a direction for WfD or ensuring coordination of effort on specific priorities.
- Under the System Oversight dimension, ensuring equitable and efficient funding for vocational education and training (VET) poses more difficulty than assuring quality or creating pathways for skills acquisition.
- Under the Service Delivery dimension, a pervasive challenge is putting in place regulations, incentives, and monitoring to ensure that training providers, both public and private, are accountable for and manage to achieve results in the job market.

Beyond the broad patterns, unpacking the dimension-level scores into their underlying drivers sheds additional light. Insofar as the distribution of low scores shows common challenges shared across emerging economies, it implies that attention, technical assistance, and exchange may be especially useful if focused on some areas more than others.

Under the Strategic Framework dimension, the findings suggest that WfD advocacy is substantive but lacks high-level advocates' sustained vocal support; that partnership with employers is weak in the absence of appropriate governance arrangements; and that effective implementation of strategic WfD tends to be neglected.

With regard to System Oversight, the findings underline the need to examine and improve equity in public spending on skills development, to destigmatize social perceptions about VET, and to strengthen program articulation to enhance options in learning pathways for skills acquisition.

Finally, under the Service Delivery dimension, the SABER-WfD findings draw attention to the potential role of performance-enhancing strategies, such as incentives as a complement to regulation in encouraging private providers to meet quality standards for service provision, performance targets in public training institutions to enhance their attention to efficiency and effectiveness, and expanded use of data for strategic management of the WfD system as a whole.

The findings generated thus far by the SABER-WfD tool illustrate its power to inform policy dialogue. The tool's conceptual framework enables a more systematic discussion of an inevitably complex topic, while its common vocabulary facilitates efficient exchange among stakeholders with diverse backgrounds, experience, and expectations, both within and across countries. The findings also suggest opportunities for supporting the development of WfD systems in emerging economies. In particular, the international development community and other partners of these economies could encourage a broadening of dialogue on WfD to engage not only educators and trainers but also key interlocutors representing employers and firms.

For most emerging economies, embedding WfD in national or regional strategies for economic growth and transformation is often also a promising way to develop and strengthen WfD systems, as experience in countries such as Ireland, Korea, and Singapore, among others, suggests. Experience also reveals that WfD systems take time to mature, highlighting the need for patient capital and sustained effort to build and consolidate the diverse components that make up WfD systems. Finally, fostering peer-to-peer learning from practitioners and encouraging policy makers to engage in experimentation and learning by doing are key avenues for reinforcing the national capacity and leadership required for success in guiding WfD systems toward maturity.

Abbreviations

ALMP	active labor market programs
ASEM	Asia-Europe Meeting
CCC	City Colleges of Chicago
CCM	Mining Skills Council (Chile)
CDC	Career Development Competency
Cedefop	European Centre for the Development of Vocational Training
CIMO	*Programa de Calidad Integral y Modernización* [Integral Quality and Modernization Program], Mexico
CVET	continuing vocational education and training
ETF	European Training Foundation
GNI	gross national income
GNP	gross national product
HRDF	Human Resources Development Fund (Malaysia)
IBRD	International Bank for Reconstruction and Development
IDA	International Development Association
ISCED	International Standard Classification of Education
ITE	Institute of Technical Education (Singapore)
IVET	initial vocational education and training
K-CESA	Korean Collegiate Essential Skills Assessment
KNCS	Korean National Competency Standards
KUT	Korea University of Technology and Education
MBO Raad	Netherlands Association of VET Colleges
MDGs	Millennium Development Goals
NOSS	National Occupational Skills Standards (Malaysia)
NQF	national qualifications framework
NUSAF	Northern Uganda Social Action Fund
OECD	Organisation for Economic Co-operation and Development
O*NET	Occupational Information Network
OTECs	*Organismos Técnicos de Capacitación* [technical training institutions] (Chile)

OTICs	*Organismos Técnicos Intermedios para Capacitación* [technical training intermediary agencies] (Chile)
PASET	Partnership for Skills in Applied Sciences, Engineering, and Technology (Africa)
PISA	Programme for International Student Assessment
P-TECH	Pathways in Technology Early College High School
SABER	Systems Approach for Better Education Results
SAR	special administration region
SDGs	Sustainable Development Goals
SENCE	National Service of Training and Employment (Chile)
SMEs	small- and medium-sized enterprises
STEP	Skills toward Employment and Productivity
UILL	UNESCO Institute of Lifelong Learning
UIS	UNESCO Institute for Statistics
UNDP	United Nations Development Programme
VET	vocational education and training
WfD	workforce development
YOP	Youth Opportunities Program (Uganda)

CHAPTER 1

Introduction

Unlike miracles, sustained high rates of economic growth can be explained and possibly replicated under certain conditions (CGD 2008). The precise recipe is elusive, but a deep fount of research in economics and other fields (e.g., Descy and Tessaring 2005; Florida, Mellander, and Stolarick 2007; Hanushek 2013; Hanushek and Woessmann 2008; Wilson and Briscoe 2004) identifies education and skills formation as an essential, if insufficient, ingredient. For emerging economies, the good news has been sufficiently persuasive to encourage decades of sustained investment in education and training. Yet evidence is also mounting that simply producing more people with higher levels of education and training may not deliver the expected results. Indeed, high and rising unemployment among educated youth around the world has put the onus on the education and training system to ensure that individuals graduate from their learning programs with the knowledge, skills, and behaviors required by employers and firms in today's globalized economy. Therefore, the spotlight is on the system's efficacy in workforce development (WfD).

This book focuses on a specific aspect of WfD: building job-relevant skills for employment and overall economic and social progress. For simplicity of exposition, the book uses the term *WfD* with this narrow meaning, even though the scope of WfD is broader. The book seeks to facilitate policy dialogue on this important development challenge, particularly between emerging countries and their development partners, as well as within countries among multiple stakeholder groups. A key objective is to clarify the nature of the problem and to highlight the need for practical, mutually reinforcing action among decision makers with diverse responsibilities in government.

The chapters draw heavily on the experience of low- and middle-income countries that have achieved sustained growth over the last few decades to highlight good practices in policies and institutions designed to bridge the gap between the supply of and demand for skills. Based on these insights, the book reflects on the implications for countries aspiring to catch up with the fast growers in their approaches to WfD. Underlying its approach is an analytical framework developed by the World Bank (2013) under the Bank's initiative on

Systems Approach for Better Education Results (SABER). The focus is on the segment of the education and training system that is closely associated with WfD, specifically most forms of vocationally oriented education and training programs at the secondary and postsecondary levels.[1] The book relies on data collected between 2010 and 2013 under the SABER initiative regarding WfD policies and institutions in 27 countries and the West Bank and Gaza.[2]

The rest of the study is organized as follows. To set the context, chapter 2 highlights trends in enrollments and learning outcomes around the world and presents patterns across countries in skills investments through multiple approaches. Chapter 3 elaborates on the challenges of policy dialogue on workforce development and proposes a framework and tool to inform and facilitate dialogue on the subject. The application of the tool for data collection is the topic of chapter 4, where key features of high-level aggregated results across countries are distilled and highlighted. Chapter 5 delves into these data in greater detail to reveal their foundations and evidence of diversity and similarities in the institutional challenges in WfD across the sample countries considered in this study. Chapter 6 concludes the book with a reflection on its findings' broader implications for policy development.

Notes

1. To keep its scope manageable, the book does not address highly specific training, particularly in higher education, geared toward the traditional occupations such as doctors, lawyers, accountants, teachers, and so forth.
2. The 27 countries include: Armenia, Bulgaria, Chile, the Arab Republic of Egypt, Georgia, Grenada, Iraq, Ireland, Jordan, the Republic of Korea, Lao People's Democratic Republic, the former Yugoslav Republic of Macedonia, Malaysia, Moldova, Morocco, Singapore, the Solomon Islands, Sri Lanka, St. Lucia, Tajikistan, Timor-Leste, Tunisia, Turkey, Uganda, Ukraine, Vietnam, and the Republic of Yemen. Among them, the following five had data for at least two years: Chile, Ireland, Korea, Malaysia, and Singapore.

References

CGD (Commission on Growth and Development). 2008. *The Growth Report: Strategies for Sustained Growth and Inclusive Development.* Washington, DC: World Bank (on behalf of the Commission on Growth and Development).

Descy, Pascaline, and Manfred Tessaring. 2005. *The Value of Learning: Evaluation and Impact of Education and Training: Third Report on Vocational Training Research in Europe: Synthesis Report.* Luxembourg: Office for Official Publications of the European Communities.

Florida, Richard, Charlotta Mellander, and Kevin Stolarick. 2008. "Inside the Black Box of Regional Development: Human Capital, the Creative Class and Tolerance." *Journal of Economic Geography* 8 (5): 615–49.

Hanushek, Eric A. 2013. "Economic Growth in Developing Countries: The Role of Human Capital." *Economics of Education Review* 37 (December): 204–12.

Hanushek, Eric A., and Ludger Woessmann. 2008. "The Role of Cognitive Skills in Economic Development." *Journal of Economic Literature* 46 (3): 607–68.

Wilson, Rob A., and Geoff Briscoe. 2004. "The Impact of Human Capital on Economic Growth: A Review." In *Impact of Education and Training: Third Report on Vocational Training Research in Europe: Background Report*, edited by Pascaline Descy and Manfred Tessaring, 9–70. Luxembourg: Office for Official Publications of the European Communities.

World Bank. 2013. "What Matters for Workforce Development: A Framework and Tool for Analysis." SABER Working Paper 6, World Bank, Washington, DC.

CHAPTER 2

Education and Skills for Growth in Emerging Economies

In both developed and emerging economies, education and skills matter for the well-being of individuals and their communities.[1] It is thus not surprising that these topics received explicit attention in the internationally agreed Millennium Development Goals for 2015, and they continue to receive attention in the follow-on agreement on Sustainable Development Goals for 2030 (UN 2014).[2] The policy challenges are complex, not least because advances in scientific knowledge and information technology are reshaping jobs and the labor market in ways that make continuous learning and adaptation an unavoidable requirement for workers in the modern workplace. As such, young people must continue to acquire skills, initially to land their first jobs and then, as labor market conditions evolve, to move on to subsequent jobs that may well point away from their initial area of expertise. In some countries the demographics of aging populations mean that even older workers, faced with the financial necessity of delayed retirement, may need new skills, again perhaps in entirely new fields, to remain economically active and productive. In dynamic labor markets, smart investments in education and skills are therefore essential for individuals and communities to thrive.

Pattern of Enrollments

Emerging economies have invested heavily in education in the last few decades and have made impressive progress. By 2010 the gross enrollment ratio for primary education in low-income countries had exceeded 100 percent, signaling attainment of coverage at levels comparable to those achieved by richer countries in earlier decades (figure 2.1). Secondary education also expanded rapidly in both low- and middle-income countries: between 1980 and 2010, the average gross enrollment ratio rose from 19 percent to 42 percent (low-income countries) and from 43 percent to 71 percent (high-income). The pattern of expansion is repeated in tertiary education: the ratio for low-income countries averaged

Figure 2.1 Gross Enrollment Ratios by Education Level and Country Income Group, 1980–2010

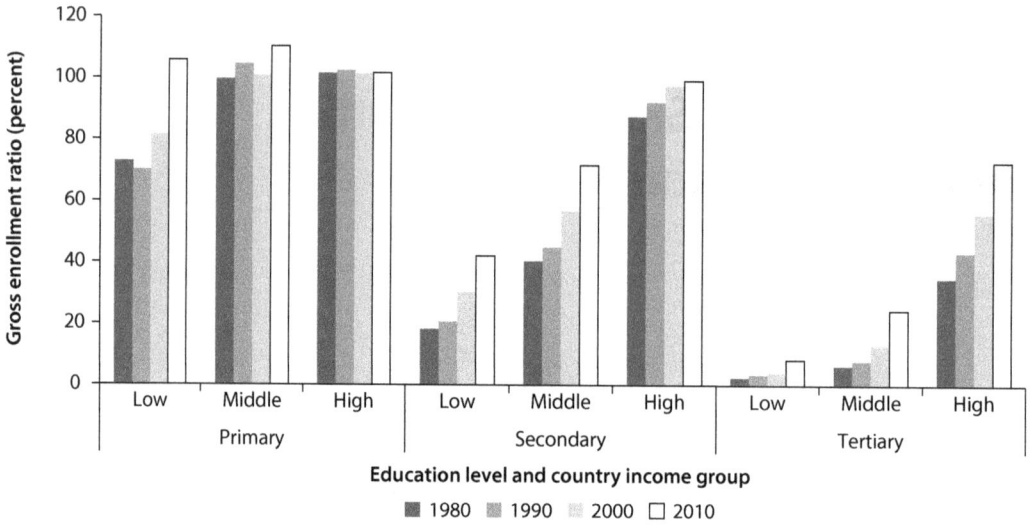

Source: World Development Indicators; World DataBank (World Bank, online). See http://databank.worldbank.org/data/views/variableselection
/selectvariables.aspx?source=world-development-indicators.
Note: Low-, middle-, and high-income countries are defined, respectively, as those with a 2013 per capita gross national income (GNI) of $1,045
or less, between $1,046 and $12,745, and above $12,746, based on World Bank data and estimates.

less than 8 percent in 2010, compared with less than 3 percent in 1980, while
the corresponding figures for middle-income countries were 28 percent and
8 percent. Youth literacy rates have risen in parallel with the expansion of education, from an average of 60 percent to 74 percent since 1980 among countries in
the first group, and from 84 percent to 91 percent among those in the latter.

The rapid expansion of coverage reflects a strong expectation that investments in education and training would yield high payoffs. A classic early study
by Easterlin (1981) concluded that no country has developed without universalizing basic education. More recent studies have refined our understanding
of the link between education and economic growth. Breton (2013) analyzes
the impact of education on the economy through direct and indirect channels,
and based on data for 2005 from 61 countries, estimates that the marginal
national return on investment in education is 12 percent in highly educated
countries and more than 50 percent in the least-educated countries. These
estimates exceed the typical direct returns to individuals, particularly in
emerging economies, and argue for public investment to capture the full
returns for the whole economy.

Cognitive, Technical, and Social-Emotional Skills

The accumulated research strongly suggests that the payoff from investments
in education depends critically on cognitive skills. Hanushek and Woessman
(2015) and Delgado, Henderson, and Parmeter (2013) show that a nation's

economic performance is linked, not to educational coverage *per se*, but to learning outcomes, which were measured in these studies by internationally comparable test scores. The role of cognitive skills has an intuitive explanation: individuals with such skills are more capable of handling and performing complex tasks and are better positioned, all else being the same, to boost the performance of their organizations and that of the economy. That there is much room for improvement in many emerging economies is evident from the results of international tests (figure 2.2).

Cognitive skills complement two other distinct skills sets—technical and social-emotional or soft skills[3]—that are also thought to matter for economic productivity. Interest in these skills sets among policy makers and researchers alike is well documented (e.g., Dundar *et al.* 2014; Harvey 2004; Heckman, Stixrud, and Urzua 2006; OECD 2012a; Pierre *et al.* 2014; Stecher and Hamilton 2014; Trilling and Fadel 2009; Wang 2012).[4] To perform tasks required in their specific jobs, people must master technical skills, such as those needed to work as a plumber, carpenter, chef, engineer, lawyer, or information technology specialist, and typically these skills are channeled through specialized protocols, standards, tools, or machines. As economies grow in sophistication, the workplace requires the performance of more complex tasks, which in turn calls for higher levels or volumes of technical skills. With regard to soft skills, their salience derives from the fact that work brings individuals into contact with others, such as colleagues, customers, and suppliers, and with situations that may require nonroutine responses, such as reacting to unexpected challenges or new opportunities. The capacity for self-regulation and interpersonal relations—which stems from personality traits, attitudes, and social skills that collectively define soft skills—affect individuals' productivity at work and often that of their coworkers as well. These skills therefore also affect the performance of firms and the broader economy. In technology-rich environments, they enable innovation and more effective ways to organize work and therefore are prized by employers (see box 2.1).

The impact of soft skills on individuals' labor market outcomes has received significant research attention in recent years, although precisely documenting it has proven elusive. Some of the research has demonstrated a causal link between soft skills and individuals' employment and earnings even after netting out the influence of cognitive skills and socioeconomic factors (e.g., Gensowski 2014; Gutman and Schoon 2013; Heckman and Kautz 2012; Prada 2013). Because soft skills can be developed later in life, a person's family background exerts less influence on their formation than it does on the formation of cognitive skills, for which the window of opportunity for development is concentrated in early childhood, and soft skills also appear to be more malleable than intelligence. These findings suggest that fostering soft skills may aid in efforts to help disadvantaged populations improve their economic well-being and their chances of escaping poverty (Gensowski 2014; Heckman and Kautz 2012; Hsin and Xie 2012; Martins 2010).

Figure 2.2 Percentage Distribution of Students by Functional Numeracy, Selected Countries

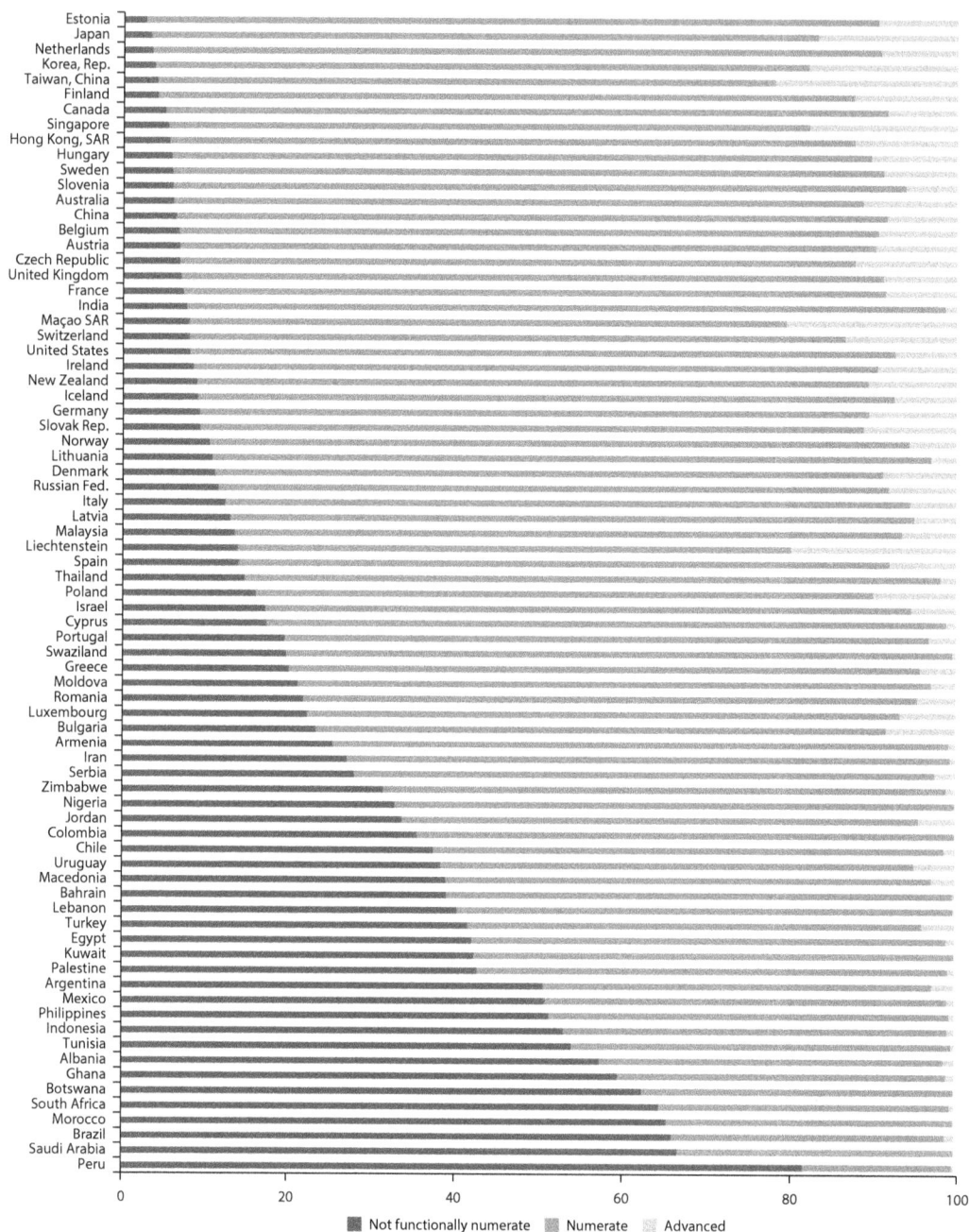

Source: Hanushek and Woessman 2006, as cited in Hanushek and Woessman 2015.

Note: The percentage distributions are based on the average score on all international tests in mathematics and science that countries participated in from 1964 to 2003. To achieve comparability across various tests, all scores were transformed to match the scale used by the Programme for International Student Assessment (PISA) tests. "Not functionally numerate" indicates a score one standard deviation below the Organisation for Economic and Co-operation and Development (OECD) mean or lower; "Advanced" indicates a score one standard deviation above the mean OECD or higher.

Box 2.1 The Importance and Broadening of Social-Emotional Skills

An extensive literature has established the importance of social-emotional or "soft" skills for individuals' career success and productivity across a wide range of economies (e.g., Blom and Saeki 2012; Cunha and Heckman 2010; Díaz, Arias, and Tudela 2013; Gutman and Schoon 2013; Heckman, Stixrud, and Urzua 2006; Nikoloski and Ajwad 2014). As the workplace has changed, so have the types of soft skills associated with higher worker productivity and remuneration.

In the late 1970s Bowles and Gintis (1976)—writing about the United States—argued that while schools play an important role in fostering cognitive skills, they also serve as an avenue for socializing students for jobs in the corporate hierarchical structures of the time. The authors highlighted the value of personality traits—such as compliance, perseverance, dependability, consistency, perseverance, punctuality, and predictability—that were especially suited for work on routine assembly lines and similar workplaces of the early to middle decades of the twentieth century, many of them run on the principles of Frederick Taylor's scientific management style (Bowles and Gintis 2002; Hartley 2012).[a]

Since the early 1980s the advent and spread of computers have altered the types of social-emotional skills desired by employers. In every industry or economic sector, computers and information technology have made it increasingly feasible and economical to automate many tasks formerly performed by humans, not only manual ones but also those that require cognitive skills (Goos 2013). This development, especially in advanced economies, has had a profound impact on how workers are organized to work productively with each other and with partially automated systems. Milgrom and Roberts (1990, 1995) and Holmstrom and Milgrom (1994) show that the adoption of lean and flexible manufacturing processes—which involve using more adaptable and programmable machines—is most successful under human resource management practices that encourage and reward skills in communication, problem solving, teamwork, creativity, and adaptability—traits that are strikingly different from those enumerated by Bowles and Gintis. Therefore, education systems today are adapting curriculums to promote such social-emotional skills, and employers have turned to strategies such as extensive screening of job applicants, increased time on training, and job rotation to select for and reinforce such skills.

Soft skills also matter for the self-employed. In emerging economies, these workers are concentrated in the informal economy. To improve productivity, they require not only technical skills to practice their trades but also a wide range of business and entrepreneurial skills, including financial management, market research, and marketing (Pina *et al*. 2012). The self-employed must also rely on themselves to a far greater degree than their formal sector counterparts. For them, possession of traits such as discipline, confidence, capacity for negotiation, communication, and decision making are invaluable, perhaps enabling them eventually to escape from being trapped in poverty in the informal economy (Pina *et al*. 2012).

a. In "Schooling in Capitalist America Revisited," Bowles and Gintis (2002) note that noncognitive skills remain important today even though the structure of the American economy has evolved since their groundbreaking analysis in 1976.

Equipping the Workforce with Job-Relevant Skills

Translating insights on the economic significance of education and skills into policies and action raises difficult practical challenges for workforce development (WfD). Immediate questions include: How do individuals acquire the desired spectrum of cognitive, technical, and behavioral skills? How are skills matched to job requirements and utilized in the workplace to achieve their impact on individual and firm productivity? What is the government's role, if any, in fostering the acquisition, matching, and utilization of skills? The issues are complex and often engage multiple parties with differing perspectives and understandings. A necessary first step is therefore to situate the discussion of WfD in an analytical framework that clarifies the key areas for action and the linkages among them.

The World Bank's (2010) Skills toward Employment and Productivity (STEP) framework offers one useful approach for conceptualizing the challenges. Workforce development in the broadest sense includes all the five policy areas discussed in box 2.2. The first three areas in the STEP framework correspond to distinct and naturally sequential stages of investment in human capital, and the last two pertain to the functioning of the labor market and to human resource practices in the workplace. All five areas are important to WfD and warrant specific attention. This paper, however, focuses on the third area—building job-relevant skills—isolating it only to contain the scope of what might otherwise be too broad a discussion. The phrase *building job-relevant skills* is used interchangeably with *WfD* in this paper, even though the STEP framework makes it clear that it is a narrower concept than WfD in its most comprehensive sense. In the rest of this chapter, we review three common approaches to building job-relevant skills: preemployment vocational education and training, workplace training, and training targeted to workers in the informal economy.

Building Job-Relevant Skills through Preemployment Training

Countries use vocational education and training (VET) as part of their institutional arrangements to build job-relevant skills. VET exists in some form in practically all countries, providing options for young people to gain job-relevant skills through organized training. VET programs typically target skilled jobs and are generally more practice-oriented than academic programs; their curricula may include soft skills training (see box 2.3).[5] Some students are tracked into VET programs as early as lower secondary school in countries as diverse as Belgium, Bulgaria, Croatia, the Lao People's Democratic Republic, Mozambique, and Tanzania. More commonly, however, VET programs are offered only after at least 9 years of general education, a practice consistent with evidence on the adverse impact of early tracking (e.g., Brunello and De Paola 2004; Hanushek and Woessmann 2006; Krueger and Kumar 2004). Even in systems with no explicit tracking, as in the United States, efforts are being made to integrate rigorous

Box 2.2 The World Bank's STEP Conceptual Framework on Skills

The Skills toward Employment and Productivity (STEP) framework identifies five broad areas for policies on skills to boost economic growth and productivity (figure B2.1). The first two areas—*getting children off to the right start* and *ensuring learning*—focus on building and reinforcing cognitive and behavioral skills early on, through early childhood development and basic education. The human capital thus created provides basic tools for individuals to continue accumulating skills, such as reading comprehension, throughout life. The third area—*building job-relevant skills*—recognizes the role of vocationally oriented investments in building skills. Such investments typically occur at the secondary and postsecondary levels through various formal and nonformal programs that may target individuals before they enter the workforce or focus on those already working. The fourth and fifth areas for action—*encouraging entrepreneurship and innovation* and *facilitating labor mobility and job matching*—shift attention to skills utilization. They recognize that economic productivity also depends on workers finding and moving to jobs that reward them for their skills and on workers being able to use their skills entrepreneurially and innovatively in the workplace.

Figure B2.1 Five Key Policy Areas on Skills for Employment and Productivity

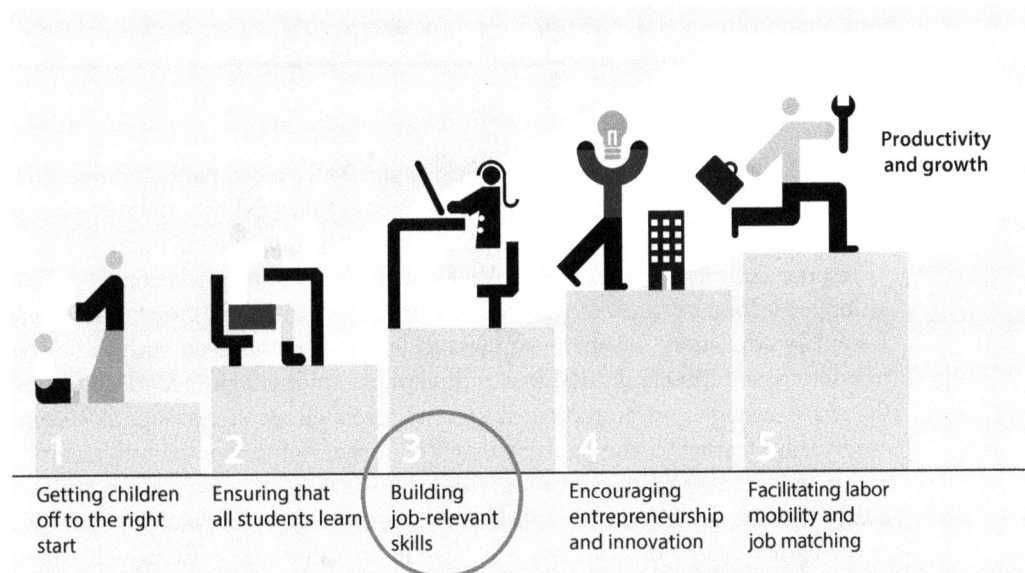

1	2	3	4	5
Getting children off to the right start	Ensuring that all students learn	Building job-relevant skills	Encouraging entrepreneurship and innovation	Facilitating labor mobility and job matching

Source: World Bank 2010.
Note: Red oval denotes this paper's focus on building job-relevant skills.

academics with career-based learning and authentic workplace experiences in professional fields such as engineering, health care, and information technology.[6] At the postsecondary level, the pathways grow in number and include instruction of varying duration offered in a range of institutions and settings, most of which culminate in certification through diplomas, degrees, and other credentials. Although significant diversity exists across countries in both the delivery

Box 2.3 Job-Relevant Soft Skills in Vocational Education and Training Programs

Training in soft skills in vocational education and training (VET) programs can take place in the classroom or in the workplace. Classroom-based approaches include simple role playing and systematic lessons from skilled instructors with built-in opportunities for practice (Bancino and Zevalkink 2005). Neither approach substitutes fully for actual workplace inter-actions, however. Internships at job sites solve this problem, but they are costly to organize and are naturally constrained by employers' reluctance or lack of capacity to host interns.

Soft skills training sometimes features in VET programs, especially those targeting disadvantaged groups; examples include Year Up in the United States (Heinrich 2012; Roder and Elliot 2011 and 2014), Jovenes programs in Latin America (González-Velosa, Ripani, and Rosas-Shady 2012), and various programs in the Middle East, North Africa, and Sub-Saharan Africa (Jayaram and Engmann 2012). The programs tend to combine classroom instruction, in both soft skills and technical or vocational subjects, and work-place experience. In the Dominican Republic, rigorous evaluation of the soft skills train-ing in the Programa Juventud y Empleo shows that this program improved some aspects of the trainees' soft skills, including self-esteem, optimism about the future, and ability to lead, self-organize, and resolve conflicts (Ibarraran *et al.* 2012).

and the duration of VET (Euler 2013; Field *et al.* 2009),[7] broad patterns in the VET share of enrollments by levels of instruction, based on UNESCO's International Standard Classification of Education (ISCED) may be discerned in figure 2.3.[8]

In poor and rich countries alike, VET's share of enrollments becomes sizable in upper-secondary and tertiary education. As figure 2.3 shows, in lower-secondary education, the share is dramatically smaller; and even with the rising trend between 2000 and 2010 that is discernible among high-income countries, the share averaged no more than 2 percent across all income groups. A second noteworthy feature in the figure is that VET's share of upper-secondary enroll-ments, in both 2000 and 2010, rises with income group. Its share was, on average, nearly three times as large in high-income countries as in low-income countries in the earlier year and about twice as large in the later year. Although the share of VET rose between 2000 and 2010 among low-income countries, the opposite trend materialized among the middle- and high-income countries. A third feature in the figure pertains to tertiary education. VET's share of tertiary enrollments no longer rises consistently with country income; indeed, by 2010 the share in high-income countries fell below that in middle-income countries. The aggregate nature of the data notwithstanding, these shifts in VET enrollments suggest greater experimentation and proactivity in high-income countries in grappling with adaptation of the education and training system to the realities of preparing youth for work in the twenty-first century (Finegold and Notabartolo 2010).[9]

Building skills through VET often requires as much, if not more, public spend-ing per student as academic programs. VET programs are costly, especially those

Figure 2.3 VET Enrollment Share by Level of Education and Country Group, 2000 and 2010

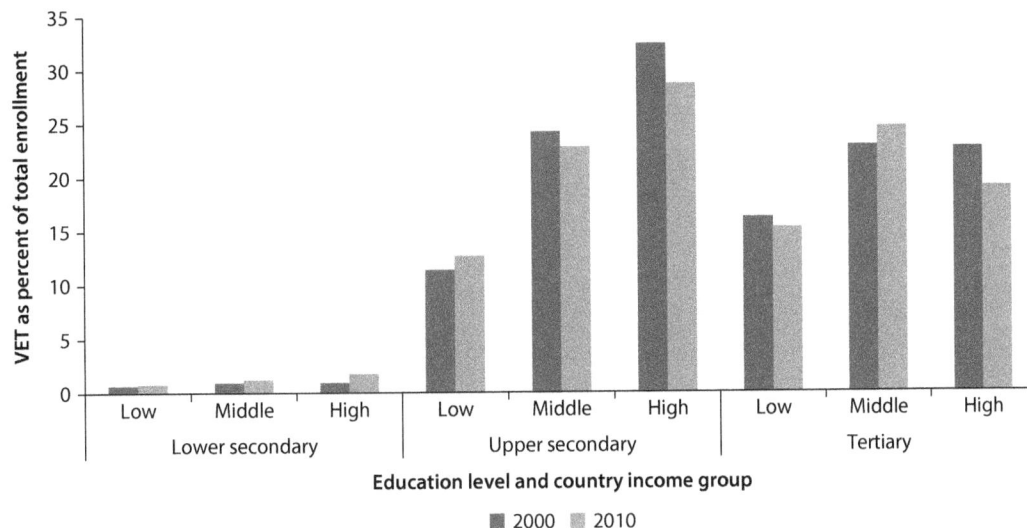

Education level and country income group

■ 2000 ▨ 2010

Source: *World Development Indicators*; World DataBank (World Bank online). See http://databank.worldbank.org/data/views/variableselection
/selectvariables.aspx?source=education-statistics-~-all-indicators.
Note: Lower secondary refers to International Standard Classification of Education (ISCED) 2; upper secondary, to ISCED 3; and tertiary, to ISCED 5B;
VET = vocational education and training.

that require heavy equipment and sophisticated infrastructure (Hoeckel 2008). Standardized data for 18 countries on public spending at the upper-secondary level generally confirms this expectation (figure 2.4). On average, spending per student is 13 percent higher for VET programs compared to academic or general education. In New Zealand, where VET provision at the upper-secondary level is primarily school-based, the public cost per VET student is 36 percent higher than that for academic or general education. In countries with a dual system, such as Germany, the Netherlands, and Switzerland, annual public spending per student is 30 percent to 60 percent higher for VET than for academic or general education. In Germany, overall public spending per student for VET, excluding apprentices' salaries, is almost twice as high as that for tertiary academic education, excluding research (Hoeckel 2008). However, the available data also indicate that higher spending on VET relative to academic programs is not universal: in countries such as Chile, Austria, and Poland, the gap is very small, while in Australia and Indonesia, government spending per student in VET is, respectively, only 40 percent and 50 percent as high as academic or general secondary education (OECD 2012b).

Links between VET and tertiary education help create flexible career pathways, enhancing job-relevant skill building. Establishing and strengthening these links is receiving sustained attention in public policy, especially in high-income countries. The effort emphasizes lifelong learning, takes many forms, and typically requires "connecting the dots" between and among institutions that may operate in silos (e.g., Schurman and Soares 2010). The aim is to offer

Figure 2.4 Per Student Public Spending on VET and Academic Programs at the Upper-Secondary Level, Selected Countries, circa 2009

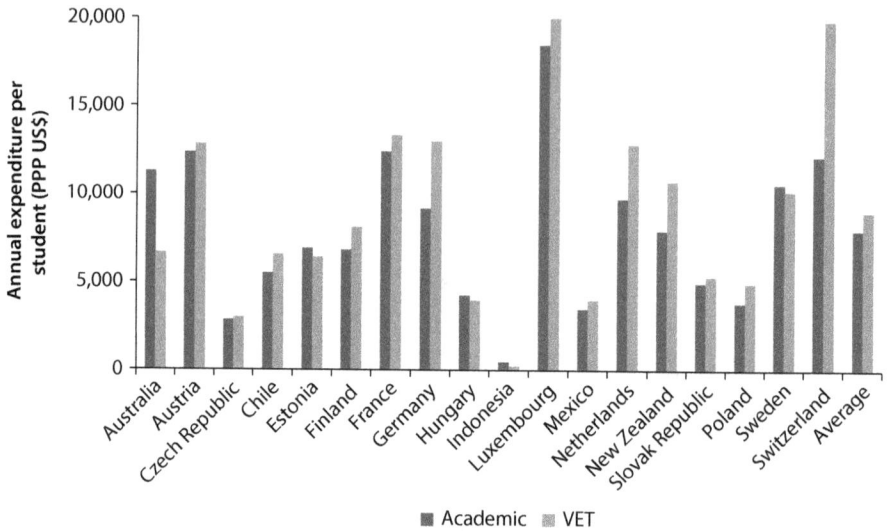

Source: OECD 2012b, table B1.6.
Note: PPP = purchasing power parity; VET = vocational education and training.

students and those already in the workforce multiple, flexible career pathways through VET and tertiary education, as visualized in figure 2.5.

An important mechanism is the facilitation of the transfer or recognition of curricula and certification credentials between different types of institutions. Non-university VET institutions may take the initiative to offer university-level courses and make their own arrangements for credit transfers to partner institutions through arrangements such as joint curriculum development or joint appointment of faculty members. More systemic arrangements often require intentional plans with a role for the government to confer special intermediate status within the tertiary education system on selected colleges (as was done for Canada's University Colleges, Mexico's Technological Universities, and Finland's Universities of Applied Sciences); to grant selected colleges a charter to upgrade to university status on a planned schedule; or to establish an independent, comprehensive quality assurance system that covers colleges and universities within the same framework for certification, as in Ireland. These measures often benefit from cultivating broader community appreciation and acceptance of VET or college credentials, notably by documenting and disseminating evidence on the employment success of VET graduates.

Building Job-Relevant Skills through Workplace Training

Workplace training—that is, training that occurs on the job—constitutes a key component of a nation's workforce development system. Its positive impact on firm productivity is well-documented around the world; yet evidence suggests

Figure 2.5 Example of Flexible Pathways for Building Job-Relevant Skills through Links between VET and Tertiary Education

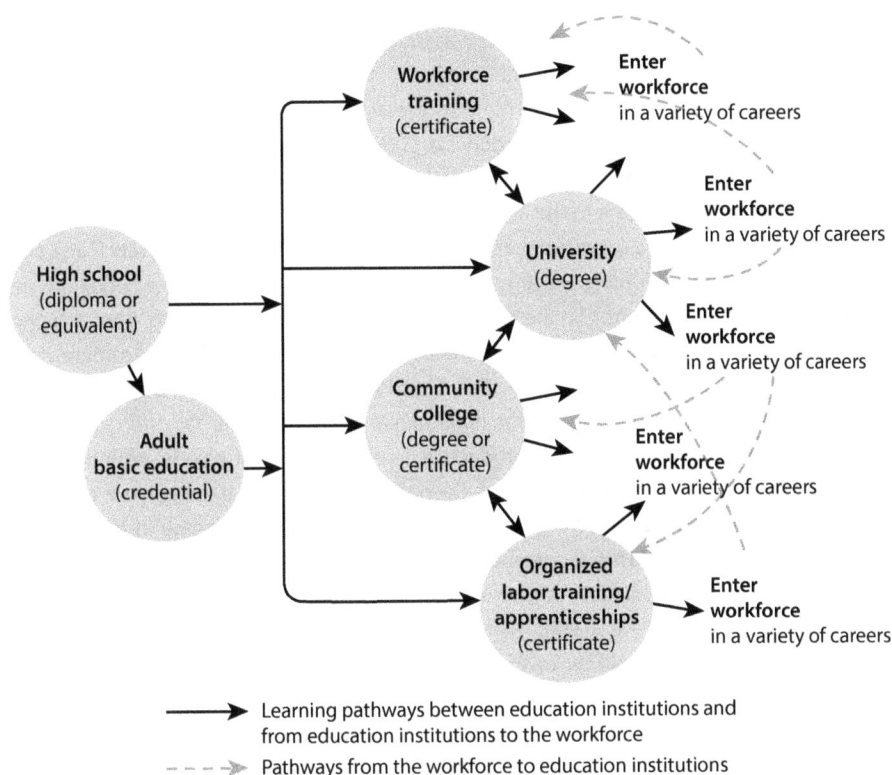

> Learning pathways between education institutions and from education institutions to the workforce
>
> - - - ▶ Pathways from the workforce to education institutions

Source: Woolsey and Groves 2013.
Note: VET = vocational education and training.

that many firms, particularly small- and medium-sized enterprises (SMEs), still do not engage systematically in building the skills of their employees (see box 2.4). Reasons for underinvestment in workplace training vary, including those revealed by the World Bank's Enterprise Surveys, which have been conducted in 135 economies since 2002. They include lack of financial resources, lack of knowledge and confidence about training benefits and options, high worker turnover, and poaching.[10] Such responses imply that underlying failures in labor and capital markets, information, and coordination may be at play (Almeida and Cho 2012). This chapter discusses government intervention to support workplace training, focusing on efforts in four areas: funding constraints, fragmentation and quality issues, lack of training expertise, and systemic coordination.

Relaxing constraints on funding can encourage training investments by small and medium enterprises (SMEs). Operated by the Ministry of Labor and Social Welfare, Mexico's CIMO (Programa de Calidad Integral y Modernización [Integral Quality and Modernization Program]) subsidizes the development and delivery of training—rather than providing direct training services—to participating firms. A key feature of this cost-sharing model is that the government defrays the

Box 2.4 Evidence on Workplace Training and Productivity

Various cross-sectional studies highlight the association between employers' investment in training and firm productivity. A study of firms in Colombia, Indonesia, Malaysia, Mexico, and Taiwan, China, confirms this relationship, with the estimated training coefficients ranging from 0.028 for Taiwan to 0.711 for Indonesia (Tan and Batra 1995). Findings from the World Business Environment Survey also reveal the impact of private training on productivity: a 10 percent marginal increase in the use of training is associated with a 0.5, 0.2, and 0.6 percentage point increase in sales growth, employment, and investment, respectively (Batra and Stone 2008). Further reinforcing the argument for workplace training, analyses of data from the World Bank's Investment Climate Surveys show that productivity gains from training range from approximately 27 percent for Colombia (1992) and India (2000) to more than 70 percent for Indonesia (1992) (Batra 2000; Tan and Batra 1995; Tan and Savchenko 2003).

In addition to cross-sectional analyses, longitudinal studies of panel data affirm the claim that firms that train are indeed more productive. In their analysis of a panel of British firms from 1983 to 1996, Dearden, Reed, and van Reenen (2000) find that training has a considerable impact on productivity. For example, a five percentage point increase in the share of trained workers in an industry is associated with a 4 percent increase in value added per worker and a 1.6 percent increase in wages. Panel studies of firms in Malaysia (Tan 2000) and Mexico (Tan and Lopez-Acevedo 2003) exhibit similar results. Firms that engage in continuous in-house training are more likely to experience greater rates of productivity growth and move into higher deciles of the wage distribution than those that make one-off or no investments in training. Explicitly incorporating such findings into practice, McBassi and Company, an investment advisory firm, created a portfolio of companies in 2001 that invest heavily in the training and development of their employees. Two additional portfolios of firms with similar missions of employee development were launched in 2003. Although causal inferences remain elusive, the results are telling: all three investment portfolios outperformed the S&P 500 by 17 percent to 35 percent in 2003 (Bassi and McMurrer 2004).

up-front costs of diagnosing CIMO's worker training needs for SMEs interested in participating in the program. The initial assessment provides the basis for identifying firm-specific constraints and for the creation of individualized training and support schemes. Furthermore, to realize economies of scale, collaboration among firms and with local service providers is emphasized (Tan and Lopez-Acevedo 2005). To provide a sense of program scope, CIMO has benefited approximately 1.6 million workers in 227,000 firms and has provided $75 million in subsidies from 2001 to 2006 (Lopez-Acevedo and Tinajero-Bravo 2013). Rigorous impact evaluations also affirm that SMEs participating in CIMO displayed greater investments in training, higher rates of capacity utilization, and increased likelihood of adopting quality practices than SMEs not involved in the program (Tan and Lopez-Acevedo 2005).

Aggregating the demand for training by SMEs assures efficient service provision and quality. Because they are modest businesses, SMEs have little time for extensive research into their training options and the quality of the available choices. Their efforts in workplace training, if conducted at all, tend to suffer from fragmentation, haphazardness, and a lack of confidence in choosing among training options. In this setting, the government can assume a critical role as convener and assurer of training quality, as exemplified by the arrangement in Chile led by the Ministry of Labor's National Service of Training and Employment (SENCE) (Galhardi 2002; Sehnbruch 2006).

Under Chile's tax rebate program—the Franquicia Tributaria—firms can reclaim up to 1 percent of the firm's payroll for training their employees. Firms can conduct their own workplace training or, if they are small, join efforts with other firms through intermediary training organizations called OTICs (Organismos Técnicos Intermedios para Capacitación [technical training intermediary agencies]) OTICs are nonprofit associations organized by economic or regional sectors and financed through membership dues from participating companies (Sehnbruch 2006). Because SENCE accepts OTIC membership dues as a legitimate claim for rebates from the Franquicia Tributaria, smaller firms have an incentive to join an OTIC and benefit from its training services. OTICs are allowed to contract for training services only from external providers known as OTECs (Organismos Técnicos de Capacitación [technical training institutions]) that are registered and authorized by SENCE and compliant with the agency's standards and regulations (Lazo 2008; Sehnbruch 2006). By playing two critical and complementary roles—aggregating demand and assuring quality—the government has created an institutional arrangement that supports investment in workplace training by SMEs.

SME access to cutting-edge training expertise requires facilitation and partnership. In the Republic of Korea, a worrisome pattern emerged revealing that despite being able to claim tax rebates against expenses incurred for worker training, far too many SMEs were still not investing in workplace training. Approximately 80 percent of large firms were claiming refunds from the Employment Insurance Fund for training and other support for employees, as compared to less than 10 percent of SMEs (Lee 2006; Lee, Seol, and Kim 2009). The stagnant picture created a dilemma for the country's leading firms as they pushed the technological frontier: either look internationally for subcontractors able to meet their demanding quality standards or work with domestic firms to upgrade workforce quality and capability. In the interest of national unity around an agenda of shared prosperity, the government facilitated a partnership model to promote the second strategy. The model involves the country's leading technology firms, their subcontractors, and the universities, all under the Employee Vocational Education Program (Lee, Seol, and Kim 2009; World Bank 2013).

The first such partnership involved Samsung and the Korea University of Technology and Education (KUT) and was launched in 2005 as the KUT Bridge Model, with the following roles for the parties: Samsung specified training content and provided experts from its staff to coteach the courses; KUT provided the training facilities and faculty; and the subcontractors released their workers for training. Because eligibility for upmarket Samsung contracts was contingent on having sufficient workers who successfully completed the training, SMEs had the incentive to participate in the program, particularly because all training costs could be claimed against the Employee Insurance Scheme. The KUT Bridge Model has been credited with raising the number of SMEs that invest in training their workers, leading the Ministry of Labor to foster its replication nationwide. Similar models are now functioning in industries such as shipbuilding, architecture, energy, and mobile telecommunications, with participation by 11 universities and major enterprises, including Hyundai Steel, MOBIS, ABB, Hanil E-Hwa, and YURA (Lee 2011).

In contrast to the foregoing examples of government intervention to address specific constraints, the Netherlands exemplifies a case in which systemic coordination of workplace training is achieved through the way training is funded. In the country's well-established and organized system of workplace training, the role of the government is simply to supply the funding. Public funding flows through two channels: employer-led sector skills councils and the MBO Raad (the Netherlands Association of VET Colleges), which represents all public colleges for secondary vocational education and training and adult education in the country (Ashton 2006).[11]

Regarding the former, government support for the sector skills councils is provided both directly, in the form of funding for training, and indirectly, through a tax refund for employers whose workplaces have been accredited by the council (Ashton 2006). Upon consultation with the unions, government funding for the skills councils is utilized in two ways: to authorize employers to receive government tax credits for training and to develop occupational standards with which all training curricula are aligned (Ashton 2006). These funds complement employers' own private contributions generated by a training levy. Approximately 0.2 percent to 0.5 percent of the wage bill, this levy contributes toward the sector training fund.

In addition to the sector skills councils, government funds are also channeled through the MBO Raad for disbursement to the vocational training colleges. These colleges provide the necessary, and typically more theoretical, off-the-job training for students as well as practical training courses for employers, who are responsible for the on-the-job component. Because curricula are aligned to the occupational standards developed by the employer-led sector skills councils, vocational colleges are able to supply employers with skilled workers who have been trained to meet their needs. As with the skills councils, government funding for the MBO Raad is supplemented by employers' private contributions provided through the council-imposed training levies. These private funds are used to pay for various one-off programs provided by the colleges.

Channeled through the sector skills councils and the MBO Raad, public funding effectively supplements private contributions to ensure a well-aligned system that is led by, and thus effectively meets, employer demands. The Netherlands' case demonstrates that when a solid institutional infrastructure is in place, the role of the government as a source of funding is critical—and appropriate—in sustaining a strong match between skills demand and supply.

Job-Relevant Skills for the Informal Economy

The size of the informal economy and concerns about social equity and poverty reduction motivate public policies aimed at raising the skills of workers in this segment of the economy. In developing countries, more than half of all nonagricultural jobs are in the informal economy; in many South Asian and Sub-Saharan African countries, the share is as high as 90 percent (Huitfeldt and Jütting 2009; ILO 2014).[12] Jobs in the informal sector employ mostly low-skilled workers and women, and typically these jobs offer modest earnings, limited security, and hardly any social protection (Adams, de Silva, and Razmara 2013; Bacchetta, Ernst, and Bustamante 2009; Palmer 2008).[13] Globalization and the spread of information technology offer opportunities for innovation, but inadequate skills may limit workers' and firms' ability to take advantage of them.[14] A full treatment of the topic can be found in publications such as Palmer (2008); Adams, de Silva, and Razmara (2013); and Walther (2013). This chapter offers some fruitful approaches for grappling with the complex issues involved.

It is important to recognize that skill gaps are just one impediment among others that depress worker and firm productivity in the informal economy. Other barriers include capital and credit constraints and poor access to technology and markets (Bacchetta, Ernst, and Bustamante 2009; Betcherman *et al.* 2007; Palmer 2008; World Bank 2006). Most informal sector entrepreneurs lack collateral to secure bank loans and must rely primarily on personal savings, money lenders, or informal arrangements with family, friends, and merchants. Borrowing costs may be higher from many of these sources, making it harder to repay and thus shrinking access to funds for their business (Blunch, Canagarajah, and Raju 2001). Framing the challenge as one of raising productivity rather than skills development may sometimes require temporarily stepping back from longer-term concerns (e.g., a weak human capital base) to act on more immediate issues, such as addressing credit market failures or enhancing business acumen and market access (Adams, de Silva, and Razmara 2013; Daniels 2010; Gaiha and Kulkarni 2013). It often also requires prioritizing investments in the skills needs of growth-oriented enterprises over those of subsistence firms (Palmer 2008).

Focusing on skills for productive work, not just on work generally, is essential if workers in the informal economy are to escape from poverty. Because most people in the informal economy are self-employed, being able to figure out where and how to locate in a value chain and being able to operate and grow well-functioning businesses are key human capital assets (Palmer 2008; Pina *et al.* 2012). Training programs that succeed in developing these skills share some common features.

First, such programs include training as part of a package of support aimed at initiating and sustaining self-employment. A good example is the Northern Uganda Social Action Fund's (NUSAF) Youth Opportunities Program (YOP), whose features include cash grants for low-income youths to receive vocational skills training and purchase tools required to practice a targeted skilled trade, encouragement for trainees to form business partnerships to manage the risk of business failure, and facilitation of access to business mentoring. Rigorous evaluation of this integrated approach confirms its positive impact on the livelihoods of YOP's participants (Blattman, Fiala, and Martinez 2014). Second, training methods, materials, and equipment must be geared to the opportunities and conditions in the informal economy; for example, where electricity is lacking or unreliable, training should teach the use of hand tools (Palmer 2008). Third, programs intended for workers in the informal economy must be highly flexible, for example, in terms of entry requirements, program duration, costs, scheduling, and financial support (Pina et al. 2012).[15]

Building on traditional apprenticeships is an appealing approach to building skills for work in the informal economy. In traditional apprenticeships, an agreement, explicit or otherwise, exists between the apprentice and the master craftsman in which the latter provides the former with largely hands-on training in exchange for a small fee, reduced wages, or both (Adams, de Silva, and Razmara 2013). A mainstay of skills development in the informal sector, the arrangement is cost-effective (ILO 2012), and often it is the only accessible and viable option for those with limited formal education and few financial means. Other attractive aspects include a focus on practical, livelihood-oriented skills and immersion in an operating enterprise that allows an observant person to pick up other complementary skills and know-how, such as customer relations and teamwork (Adams, de Silva, and Razmara 2013; Haan 2002; Pina et al. 2012). Sometimes, graduating apprentices acquire sufficient knowledge and skills to set up shop near the master craftsman, thereby creating a cluster of similar informal businesses; Kenya's *Jua Kali* cluster is an example of the process (Daniels 2010).

Traditional apprenticeships have important drawbacks, however. First, most of the skills taught are often rudimentary, light on theory, and limited by the master craftsman's own knowledge, tools, and technologies; they therefore do little to enable workers to move to more productive work, or to boost their productivity and wages (Adams, de Silva, and Razmara 2013; Pina et al. 2012; Walther 2008). Some countries, such as Côte d'Ivoire, Mali, Senegal, and Tanzania, address this issue through "dual apprenticeships" that combine school-based education with practical on-the-job training provided by master craftsmen (Pina et al. 2012; Walther 2008). A second drawback is that master craftsmen depend on their skills to make a living, and they may have weak incentives to impart their skills to apprentices in an efficient or comprehensive manner (World Bank 2008). Benin's comprehensive approach to strengthening its system of traditional apprenticeships (box 2.5) recognizes this problem and addresses it through subsidized skills-upgrading for master craftsmen, who sign up as trainers in the country's dual apprenticeship system (Haan and Serrière 2002; ILO 2012).

Strengthening the evaluation of skills initiatives in the informal economy is critical for enhancing the initiatives' focus and design. Most programs seek to equip trainees with skills for productive work, but too few are routinely evaluated for impact (Adams et al. 2013; Palmer 2008; Tripney and Hombrados 2013). As a result, feedback is limited on how to improve program design or

Box 2.5 Benin's Dual Apprenticeship System

In 2001 Benin reformed its traditional apprenticeship system with the introduction of new training curricula that emphasized both theory and practice (ILO 2012).[a] Implementation of the new dual apprenticeship system involved trade associations representing master crafts-people as well as a consortium of reputable public and private training providers. These parties collaborated on matters such as design of new training modules, training delivery and quality assurance, trainee selection, negotiation of instructors' fees, monitoring of trainee attendance, specification and implementation of assessments, and program evaluation (ILO 2008a). A payroll levy on registered enterprises was put in place to fund the system. Funding stability remains elusive, however, as responsibility for collecting the levy rests with the Treasury, which is not obligated to send along the entire collection to the Fonds de Développement de la Formation Continue et de l'Apprentissage, which manages the training fund (ILO 2012; Johanson 2009; Walther and Uhder 2015).

Evaluation of Benin's dual apprenticeship system nonetheless shows that it has had a positive impact. Trainees with only primary education were able to pass formal trade tests at the end of their training; some of them even qualified for the *Certificat d'Aptitude Professionnelle*, an award based on tests normally taken by students in formal vocational pro-grams at the secondary level. More important, employers were more likely to hire graduates of the dual apprenticeship program than other job candidates (ILO 2008b; Walther and Filipiak 2007). Among craft workers who received training, 60 percent reported subsequent increases in turnover and profits, 70 percent had entered new markets, and more than 80 percent felt that the training had improved their technical knowledge (Walther and Filipiak 2006).

Several factors contributed to Benin's successful reform. It gave traditional apprenticeships a role and offered master craftspeople opportunities to upgrade their own skills in the system. The process of curriculum development, course delivery, and skills testing was systematic and involved not only training providers but also representatives from government, business organizations, trade groups, and parents' associations. Significant effort was made to engage the relevant stakeholders in strategic decision making, notably the National Federation of Craftsmen (Fédération nationale des Artisans du Bénin), key employer groups, and trade unions. Interministerial consultation and coordination within government facilitated the leg-islative and regulatory measures required for the reform to succeed. Involvement of local craft worker groups ensured smooth implementation of the agreed measures. In addition, regular monitoring tracked progress and verified it through periodic site visits by supervisors (ILO 2012; Walther and Filipiak 2006, 2007).

a. As in most poor countries with large informal economies, Benin's traditional apprenticeships provided a common avenue for skills acquisition. The training was almost entirely hands-on, with apprentices performing manual tasks specified by the master craftsman, and it typically did not lead to formal certification of the skills acquired.

prioritize funding for the more effective programs. Operational flaws often persist, including problems such as a focus on certification for formal sector jobs that may not materialize, too much weight on theoretical instruction at the expense of hands-on learning, and inattention to the role of key partners, such as master craftsmen and employers, in trainee selection, curriculum design, and the delivery of lessons.[16] A more systematic approach to evaluation is essential to avoid wasting resources on ineffective programs. Fortunately, the growing availability of tools and resources for impact evaluation makes it as feasible as it is attractive.[17]

Notes

1. See, for example, World Bank (2012a,b) and OECD (2015) for recent evidence that provides compelling support for the importance of investing in education and skills in both poor and rich countries.

2. The Sustainable Development Goals for 2030—adopted by heads of state and government and high representatives, at their September 2015 meeting at the United Nations in New York—make explicit mention of vocational education and training, in contrast to the Millennium Development Goals for 2015, which do not; for more information on the SDGs, see https://sustainabledevelopment.un.org/post2015/transformingourworld.

3. Terms such as *behavioral skills, character skills, life skills, noncognitive abilities, personality traits*, and *21st century skills* are also widely used in the literature (Gutman and Schoon 2013; Heckman and Kautz 2012).

4. Making a three-part distinction among cognitive, technical, and social-emotional skills is a common approach. It is used, for example, in the World Bank's multicountry surveys of skills in emerging economies under the STEP (Skills toward Employment and Productivity) initiative (Pierre *et al.* 2014). The distinction resonates with the Data-Things-People taxonomy in the *Dictionary of Occupational Titles*, a precursor to the U.S. Department of Labor's current Occupational Information Network (O*NET), a comprehensive information system on occupational characteristics and worker attributes. The taxonomy is based on the premise that all jobs require workers to relate, to varying degrees, to data, things, and people, and that distinct skills sets affect the effectiveness of these relationships in the workplace (Harvey 2004).

5. The differentiation between academic and vocationally oriented training is not watertight, however. In some professions, such as medicine, course content contains significant theoretical and practical components.

6. Examples include California's Linked Learning initiative, which has ongoing pilots in 63 districts, based on positive evaluations of previous pilots (see http://linkedlearning.org/about/; and Pathways in Technology Early College High School (P-TECH) in New York State (see http://www.aspeninstitute.org/policy-work/economic-opportunities/skills-americas-future/models-success/ibm.

7. The Netherlands, for example, offers dual- and school-based VET programs of one and four years; in Denmark, 30 percent of tenth grade completers receive six months of school-based basic VET in one of 12 fields before continuing to train in some 120 skilled occupations that typically involve alternating periods of school- and company-based instruction (Euler 2013).

8. To be consistent with the data available at the time of this writing, the figure uses the 1997 ISCED classification; see UNESCO (2012) for the most recent ISCED classification.

9. In the United States, for example, some have advocated for four-year college education for all young people, others have pushed for more diversified approaches, and still others for lengthening ISCED 5B training programs and intensifying their theoretical

content (Gitterman and Coclanis 2012; Manyika *et al.* 2012) Examples of the new types of ISCED 5B programs include those offered by Kettering University (formerly GM Institute) and the Franklin W. Olin College of Engineering. A Manufacturing Universities Act was proposed in 2014 aimed at founding 20 manufacturing universities.

10. For details on the surveys, see http://www.enterprisesurveys.org/.

11. The MBO Raad was formerly known as the BVE Raad (Keating 2008); see also http://www.mboraad.nl/?page/530112/About+us.aspx 2009.

12. In Sub-Saharan Africa, the informal sector accounts for nearly 70 percent of employment outside farming (Adams, de Silva, and Razmara 2013).

13. Many in the informal sector workforce consist of own-account workers displaced involuntarily from the formal sector; the evidence points to rising numbers of informal wage workers and greater insecurity among such workers (Carr and Chen 2002; Daniels 2010).

14. Large retailers, for example, prioritize just-in-time production, which in fast-paced markets (e.g., fashion-oriented apparel) implies a preference for informal work arrangements and piecework by suppliers (Carr and Chen 2002). Information technology, by enabling remote working and the fragmentation, distribution, and aggregation of tasks across space and time, encourages microwork (a sort of piecework in the information technology sector) and other informal jobs (e.g., Jayaram, Hill, and Plaut 2013; Monitor Group 2011).

15. Such flexibility must be closely monitored, however. For example, shorter programs may reduce costs, but they may also produce "half-baked" graduates who lack the minimum competence to practice their trade, an ever-present risk where entering trainees lack prior trade knowledge (Johanson and Adams 2004; Palmer 2008).

16. An example of failure to involve key stakeholders was the selection of apprentices for the Nigerian Open Apprenticeship Scheme. Because it was managed entirely by the National Directorate of Employment, master craftsmen in the scheme played no role and therefore took little responsibility for training outcomes (Palmer 2008).

17. Descy and Tessaring (2005) discuss a variety of approaches and methods of program evaluation and impact research from Cedefop background reports; Billorou, Pacheco, and Vargas (2011) produced a practical guide to conducting impact evaluations of skills development programs, which takes into account developing country contexts and organizations that are responsible for skills development.

References

Adams, Arvil V., Sara Johansson de Silva, and Setareh Razmara. 2013. *Improving Skills Development in the Informal Sector*. Washington, DC: World Bank.

Almeida, Rita, and Yoonyoung Cho. 2012. "Employer-Provided Training: Patterns and Incentives for Building Skills for Higher Productivity." In *The Right Skills for the Job? Rethinking Effective Training Policies for Workers*, edited by Rita Almeida, Jere Behrman, and David Robalino, 105–32. Washington, DC: Social Protection, Human Development Network, World Bank.

Ashton, David. 2006. "Lessons from Abroad: Developing Sector Based Approaches to Skills." *SSDA Catalyst* 2. Published by the Sector Skills Development Agency, Wath-upon-Dearne, England.

Bacchetta, Marc, Ekkehard Ernst, and Juana P. Bustamante. 2009. *Globalization and Informal Jobs in Developing Countries.* Geneva: International Labour Office and World Trade Organization.

Bancino, Randy, and Claire Zevalkink. 2005. "Soft Skill: The Skills for the Job." *Techniques,* May. Alexandria, VA: Association for Career and Technical Education.

Bassi, Laurie, and Dan McMurrer. 2004. "How's Your Return on People?" *Harvard Business Review* 82 (March): 18.

Batra, Geeta. 2000. "Foreign Direct Investment and Skills Upgrading in Developing Countries." World Bank: Foreign Investment Advisory Service, Washington, DC.

Batra, Geeta, and Andrew H. W. Stone. 2008. "Investment Climate, Capabilities and Firm Performance: Evidence from the World Business Environment Survey." *OECD Journal: General Papers* 6 (1): 1–35.

Betcherman, Gordon, Martin Godfrey, Susana Puerto, Friederike Rother, and Antoneta Stavreska. 2007. "A Review of Interventions to Support Young Workers: Findings of the Youth Employment Inventory." SP Discussion Paper 0715, Social Protection, World Bank, Washington, DC.

Billorou, Nina, Martha Pacheco, and Fernando Vargas. 2011. *Skills Development Impact Evaluation: A Practical Guide.* Montevideo: International Labour Organization (ILO/ Cinterfor).

Blattman, Christopher, Nathan Fiala, and Sebastian Martinez. 2014. "Generating Skilled Self-Employment in Developing Countries: Experimental Evidence from Uganda." *Quarterly Journal of Economics* 129 (2): 697–752.

Blom, Andreas, and Hiroshi Saeki. 2012. "Employability and Skill Sets of Newly Graduated Engineers in India: A Study. *IUP Journal of Soft Skills* 6 (4): 7–50.

Blunch, Niels-Hugo, Sudharshan Canagarajah, and Dhushyanth Raju. 2001. "The Informal Sector Revisited: A Synthesis Across Space and Time." Social Protection Discussion Paper 0119, Social Protection Unit, Human Development Network, World Bank, Washington, DC.

Bowles, Samuel, and Herbert Gintis. 1976. *Schooling in Capitalist America: Educational Reform and the Contradictions of Economic Life.* New York: Basic Books.

———. 2002. "Schooling in Capitalist America Revisited." *Sociology of Education* 75 (1): 1–18.

Breton, Theodore R. 2013. "The Role of Education in Economic Development: Theory, History, and Current Returns." *Educational Research* 55 (2): 121–38.

Brunello, Giorgio, and Maria De Paola. 2004. "Market Failures and the Under-Provision of Training." CESifo Working Paper 1286, Center for Economic Studies, Ludwig Maximilian University of Munich, Munich.

Carr, Marilyn, and Martha Alter Chen. 2002. "Globalization and the Informal Economy: How Global Trade and Investment Impact on the Working Poor." Working Paper on the Informal Economy 2002/1, Employment Sector, International Labour Office, Geneva.

Cunha, Flavio, and James J. Heckman. 2010. "Investing in Our Young People." Working Paper 16201, National Bureau of Economic Research, Cambridge, MA.

Daniels, Steve. 2010. *Making Do: Innovation in Kenya's Informal Economy.* San Francisco: Creative Commons Attribution.

Dearden, Lorraine, Howard Reed, and John van Reenen. 2000. "Who Gains When Workers Train? Training and Corporate Productivity in a Panel of British Industries." IFS Working Paper 00/04, Institute for Fiscal Studies, London.

Delgado, Michael S., Daniel J. Henderson, and Christopher F. Parmeter. 2013. "Does Education Matter for Economic Growth?" *Oxford Bulletin of Economics and Statistics* 76 (3): 334–59.

Descy, Pascaline, and Manfred Tessaring. 2005. *The Value of Learning: Evaluation and Impact of Education and Training: Third Report on Vocational Training Research in Europe: Synthesis Report.* Luxembourg: Office for Official Publications of the European Communities.

Díaz, Juan José, Omar Arias, and David Vera Tudela. 2013. "Does Perseverance Pay as Much as Being Smart? The Returns to Cognitive and Non-cognitive Skills in Urban Peru." Unpublished, World Bank, Washington, DC.

Dundar, Halil, Benoît Millot, Yevgeniya Savchenko, Harsha Aturupane, and Tilkaratne A. Piyasiri. 2014. *Building the Skills for Economic Growth and Competitiveness in Sri Lanka.* Directions in Development. Washington, DC: World Bank.

Easterlin, Richard A. 1981. "Why Isn't the Whole World Developed?" *Journal of Economic History* 41 (1): 1–17.

Euler, Dieter. 2013. *Germany's Dual Vocational Training System: A Model for Other Countries?* Gütersloh: Bertelsmann Stiftung.

Field, Simon, Kathrin Hoeckel, Viktória Kis, and Malgorzata Kuczera. 2009. *Learning for Jobs: OECD Policy Review of Vocational Education and Training: Initial Report.* Paris: OECD Publishing.

Finegold, David, and Alexis Spencer Notabartolo. 2010. "21st-Century Competencies and Their Impact: An Interdisciplinary Literature Review." In *Transforming the U.S. Workforce Development System: Lessons from Research and Practice* edited by David Finegold, Mary Gatta, Hal Salzman, and Susan J. Schurman, 19–56. Ithaca, NY: ILR Press.

Gaiha, Raghav, and Vani S. Kulkarni. 2013. "Credit, Microfinance and Empowerment." Paper presented at the Export Group Meeting: Policies and Strategies to Promote Empowerment of People in Achieving Poverty Eradication, Social Integration and Full Employment and Decent Work for All, September 10–11, United Nations Secretariat, New York.

Galhardi, Regina M. A. A. 2002. "Financing Training: Innovative Approaches in Latin America." EMP/SKILLS Working Paper 12, International Labour Organization, Geneva.

Gensowski, Miriam. 2014. "Personality, IQ, and Lifetime Earnings." IZA Discussion Paper 8235, Forschungsinstitut zur Zukunft der Arbeit (Institute for the Study of Labor), Bonn.

Gitterman, Daniel P., and Peter A. Coclanis. 2012. *Moving beyond Plato versus Plumbing: Individualized Education and Career Passways for All North Carolinians.* Chapel Hill: Global Research Institute, University of North Carolina.

González-Velosa, Carolina, Laura Ripani, and David Rosas-Shady. 2012. "How Can Job Opportunities for Young People in Latin America Be Improved?" Inter-American Development Bank Technical Note 345, Inter-American Development Bank, Washington, DC.

Goos, Maarten. 2013. "How the World of Work Is Changing: A Review of the Evidence." International Labour Office, Bureau for Employers' Activities, Geneva.

Gutman, Leslie Morrison, and Ingrid Schoon. 2013. *The Impact of Non-cognitive Skills on Outcomes for Young People: Literature Review*. London: Institute of Education, University of London and Education Endowment Fund.

Haan, Hans Christiaan. 2002. "Training for Work in the Informal Sector: New Evidence from Eastern and Southern Africa." Occasional Paper (November 2001), International Training Centre of the International Labour Organization, Turin.

Haan, Hans Christiaan, and Nicolas Serrière. 2002. "Training for Work in the Informal Sector: Fresh Evidence from West and Central Africa." Occasional Paper (August 2002), International Training Centre of the International Labour Organization, Turin.

Hanushek, Eric A., and Ludger Woessmann. 2006. "Does Educational Tracking Affect Performance and Inequality? Differences-in-Differences Evidence across Countries." *Economic Journal* 116 (150): C63–C76.

———. 2015. *The Knowledge Capital of Nations: Education and the Economics of Growth*. CESifo Series. Cambridge, MA: MIT Press.

Hartley, David. 2012. *Education and the Culture of Consumption: Personalisation and the Social Order*. Abingdon, UK: Routledge.

Harvey, Robert J. 2004. "Empirical Foundations for the Things-Data-People Taxonomy of Work." Paper presented at the Annual Conference of the Society for Industrial and Organizational Psychology: Things, Data, and People: Fifty Years of a Seminal Theory, Chicago, April.

Heckman, James J., and Tim Kautz. 2012. "Hard Evidence on Soft Skills." IZA Discussion Paper 6580, Forschungsinstitut zur Zukunft der Arbeit (Institute for the Study of Labor), Bonn.

Heckman, James J., Jora Stixrud, and Sergio Urzua. 2006. "The Effects of Cognitive and Noncognitive Abilities on Labor Market Outcomes and Social Behavior." *Journal of Labor Economics* 24 (3): 411–82.

Heinrich, Carolyn. 2012. "How Does Year Up Measure Up?" *Focus* 29 (2): 13–15.

Hoeckel, Kathrin. 2008. *Costs and Benefits in Vocational Education and Training*. Paris: OECD Publishing.

Holmstrom, Bengt, and Paul Milgrom. 1994. "The Firm as an Incentive System." *American Economic Review* 84 (4): 972–91.

Hsin, Amy, and Yu Xie. 2012. "Hard Skills, Soft Skills: The Relative Roles of Cognitive and Non-cognitive Skills in Intergenerational Social Mobility." PSC Research Report 12–755, Population Studies Center, University of Michigan, Ann Arbor.

Huitfeldt, Henrik, and Johannes Jütting. 2009. "Informality and Informal Employment." In *Promoting Pro-poor Growth: Employment*, edited by Angela Stuart, 95–108. Development Assistance Committee (DAC) Network on Poverty Reduction. Paris: OECD Publishing.

Ibarraran, Pablo, Laura Ripani, Bibiana Taboada, Juan Miguel Villa, and Brigida Garcia. 2012. "Life Skills, Employability and Training for Disadvantaged Youth: Evidence from a Randomized Evaluation Design." IZA Discussion Paper 6615, Forschungsinstitut zur Zukunft der Arbeit (IZA, Institute for the Study of Labor), Bonn.

ILO (International Labour Office). 2008a. "Skills for Improved Productivity, Employment Growth and Development." Report V, International Labour Conference, 97th Session. International Labour Office, Geneva.

————. 2008b. "Apprenticeship in the Informal Economy in Africa." Employment Report No.1, Employment Sector, International Labour Office, Geneva.

————. 2012. *Upgrading Informal Apprenticeship: A Resource Guide for Africa*. Geneva: International Labour Organization.

————. 2014. *Global Employment Trends 2014: Risk of a Jobless Recovery?* Geneva: International Labour Organization.

Jayaram, Shubha, and Michelle Engmann. 2012. *Public Sector Initiatives to Support Skills Development*. Washington, DC: Results for Development Institute.

Jayaram, Shubha, Tara Hill, and Daniel Plaut. 2013. *Training Models for Employment in the Digital Economy*. Washington, DC: Results for Development Institute.

Johanson, Richard. 2009. "A Review of National Training Funds." Social Protection Discussion Paper 0922, Social Protection and Labor, World Bank, Washington, DC.

Johanson, Richard K., and Arvil V. Adams. 2004. *Skills Development in Sub-Saharan Africa*. Washington, DC: World Bank.

Keating, Jack. 2008. *Matching Supply of and Demand for Skills: International Perspectives*. Adelaide, Australia: National Centre for Vocational Education Research.

Krueger, Dick, and Krishna B. Kumar. 2004. "Skill-Specific Rather than General Education: A Reason for US-Europe Growth Differences." *Journal of Economic Growth* 9 (2): 167–205.

Lazo, Pablo. 2008. "The Role of Technical and Vocational Education and Training Providers (TVET Providers) in Training for Employees." Paper presented at the APEC Forum on Human Resources Development 2008: The Role of TVET Providers in Training for Employees, Chiba, November 19–21.

Lee, Kye Woo. 2006. "Effectiveness of Government's Occupational Skills Development Strategies for Small- and Medium-Scale Enterprises: A Case Study of Korea." *International Journal of Educational Development* 26 (3): 278–94.

Lee, Wooyoung. 2011. "A BRIDGE Model of University-Industry Cooperation to Develop Skills of Practical Engineers for Small-Medium Companies." PowerPoint presentation for the visiting World Bank team, Korea University of Technology and Education, Cheon-An, November.

Lee, Wooyoung, Jinsoo Seol, and Jinwoo Kim. 2009. "A BRIDGE Model of University-Industry Cooperation to Develop Skills of Practical Engineers for Small-Medium Companies." Unpublished paper, Korea University of Technology and Education, Cheon-An.

Lopez -Acevedo, Gladys, and Monica Tinajero -Bravo. 2013. "Evaluating Different Types of Enterprise Support Programs Using Panel Firm Data: Evidence from the Mexican Manufacturing Sector." *Economia* 14 (1): 1–26.

Manyika, James, Jeff Sinclair, Richard Dobbs, Gernot Strube, Louis Rassey, Jan Mischke, Jaana Remes, Charles Roxburgh, Katy George, David O'Halloran, and Sreenivas Ramaswamy. 2012. *Manufacturing the Future: The Next Era of Global Growth and Innovation*. New York: McKinsey Global Institute.

Martins, Pedro S. 2010. "Can Targeted, Non-cognitive Skills Programs Improve Achievement? Evidence from EPIS." IZA Discussion Paper 5266, Forschungsinstitut zur Zukunft der Arbeit (Institute for the Study of Labor), Bonn.

Milgrom, Paul, and John Roberts. 1990. "The Economics of Modern Manufacturing: Technology, Strategy, and Organization." *American Economic Review* 80 (3): 511–28.

———. 1995. "Complementarities and Fit: Strategy, Structure and Organizational Change in Manufacturing." *Journal of Accounting and Economics* 19 (2–3): 179–208.

Monitor Group. 2011. "Job Creation through Building the Field of Impact Sourcing." Monitor Ideas Working Paper (June), Monitor Group and Rockefeller Foundation, Mumbai.

Nikoloski, Zlatko, and Mohamed Ihsan Ajwad. 2014. "Cognitive and Non-cognitive Skills Affect Employment Outcomes: Evidence from Central Asia." Paper presented at the IZA/OECD/World Bank Workshop on Cognitive and Non-cognitive Skills Development, Centro Residenziale Universitario di Bertinoro, Bertinoro, October 3–4.

OECD (Organisation for Economic Co-operation and Development). 2012a. *Better Skills, Better Jobs, Better Lives: A Strategic Approach to Skills Policies*. Paris: OECD Publishing.

———. 2012b. *Education at a Glance 2012: OECD Indicators*. Paris: OECD Publishing.

———. 2015. "Skills beyond School: Synthesis Report." *OECD Reviews of Vocational Education and Training*. Paris: OECD Publishing.

Palmer, Robert. 2008. "Skills and Productivity in the Informal Economy." Employment Working Paper 5, Employment Sector, International Labour Office, Geneva.

Pierre, Gaëlle, Maria Laura Sanchez Puerta, Alexandria Valerio, and Tania Rajadel. 2014. "STEP Skills Measurement Surveys: Innovative Tools for Assessing Skills." Social Protection and Labor Discussion Paper 1421, Social Protection and Labor, World Bank, Washington, DC.

Pina, Patricia, Tim Kotin, Vicky Hausman, and Edwin Macharia. 2012. "Skills for Employability: The Informal Economy." Paper prepared for the Innovative Secondary Education for Skills Enhancement (ISESE), Results for Development Institute, Washington, DC.

Prada, Maria F. 2013. "Beyond Smart and Sociable: Rethinking the Role of Abilities on Occupational Choices." Paper presented at the 76th International Atlantic Economic Conference, Philadelphia, October 10–13.

Roder, Anne, and Mark Elliott. 2011. *A Promising Start: Year Up's Initial Impacts on Low-Income Young Adults' Careers*. New York: Economic Mobility Corporation.

———. 2014. *Sustained Gains: Year Up's Continued Impact on Young Adults' Earning*. New York: Economic Mobility Corporation.

Schurman, Susan, and Louis Soares. 2010. "Connecting the Dots: Creating a Postsecondary Education System for the 21st-Century Workforce." In *Transforming the U.S. Workforce Development System: Lessons from Research and Practice*, edited by David Finegold et al., 125–52. Ithaca, NY: ILR Press.

Sehnbruch, Kirsten. 2006. *The Chilean Labor Market: A Key to Understanding Latin American Labor Markets*. New York: Palgrave Macmillan.

Stecher, Brian M., and Laura S. Hamilton. 2014. *Measuring Hard-to-Measure Student Competencies: A Research and Development Plan*. Santa Monica: Rand Corporation.

Tan, Hong W. 2000. *Malaysia Skill Needs Study*. Washington, DC: World Bank Institute.

Tan, Hong W., and Geeta Batra. 1995. "Enterprise Training in Development Countries: Overview of Incidence, Determinants, and Productivity Outcomes." Occasional Paper 9, Private Sector Development Department, World Bank, Washington, DC.

Tan, Hong W., and Gladys Lopez-Acevedo. 2003. "Mexico: In-Firm Training for the Knowledge Economy." Policy Research Working Paper 2957, World Bank, Washington, DC.

————. 2005. "Evaluating Training Programs for Small and Medium Enterprises: Lessons from Mexico." Policy Research Working Paper 3760, World Bank, Washington, DC.

Tan, Hong. W., and P. Savchenko. 2003. *In-Service Training and Productivity: Results from Investment Climate Surveys.* Washington, D.C.: World Bank.

Trilling, Bernie, and Charles Fadel. 2009. *21st Skills: Learning for Our Times, Partnership for 21st Century Skills.* San Francisco: John Wiley and Sons.

Tripney, Janice S., and Jorge Hombrados. 2013. "Technical and Vocational Education and Training (TVET) for Young People in Low- and Middle-Income Countries: A Systematic Review and Meta-analysis." *Empirical Research in Vocational Education and Training* 5 (3): 1–14.

UN (United Nations). 2014. "Open Working Group Proposal for Sustainable Development Goals." http://www.un.org/ga/search/view_doc.asp?symbol=A/68/970.

UNESCO Institute for Statistics (UIS). 2012. *International Standard Classification of Education: ISCED 2011.* Montreal: UNESCO Institute for Statistics.

Walther, Richard. 2008. *Towards a Renewal of Apprenticeship in West Africa: Enhancing the Professional Integration of Young People.* Paris: Agence Française de Développement.

————. 2013. "Building Skills in the Informal Sector." In *Technical and Vocational Skills Development in the Informal Sector*, edited by Karen Langer, 19–28. Bonn: Institut für Internationale Zusammenarbeit des Deutschen Volkshochschul-Verbandes.

Walther, Richard, and Ewa Filipiak. 2006. "Vocational Training in the Informal Sector: Report on the Benin Field Study." AFD Working Paper 19, Agence Française de Développement, Paris.

————. 2007. *Vocational Training in the Informal Sector or How to Stimulate the Economies of Developing Countries? Conclusions of a Field Survey in Seven African Countries.* Paris: Agence Française de Développement.

Walther, Richard, and Christine Uhder. 2015. *The Financing of Vocational Training in Africa: Roles and Specificities of Vocational Training Funds.* Paris: Agence Française de Développement.

Wang, Yidan. 2012. *Education in a Changing World: Flexibility, Skills, and Employability.* Washington, DC: World Bank.

Woolsey, Lindsey, and Garrett Groves. 2013. *State Sector Strategies Coming of Age: Implications for State Workforce Policymakers.* Washington, DC: National Governors Association Center for Best Practices.

World Bank. 2006. *World Development Report 2007: Development and the Next Generation.* Washington, DC.

————. 2008. "Skills Development in India: The Vocational Education and Training System." South Asia Human Development Sector Report 22, Human Development Unit, South Asia Region, World Bank, Washington, DC.

————. 2010. *Stepping Up Skills for More Jobs and Higher Productivity.* Washington, DC.

————. 2012a. *World Development Report 2013: Jobs.* World Bank, Washington, DC.

————. 2012b. *Youth Employment Programs: An Evaluation of World Bank and International Finance Corporation Support.* Washington, DC: Independent Evaluation Group, World Bank.

————. 2013. "What Matters for Workforce Development: A Framework and Tool for Analysis." SABER Working Paper 6, World Bank, Washington, DC.

CHAPTER 3

A Framework and Tool for Dialogue on Workforce Development

Policy dialogue on workforce development (WfD) presents unique challenges. Unlike the other four areas considered in the Skills toward Employment and Productivity (STEP) framework (see box 2.2, page 11), building job-relevant skills arguably requires a more intentional engagement by multiple stakeholders from diverse sectors. In all three approaches to WfD discussed in chapter 2— preemployment vocational education and training (VET), workplace training, and training for the informal economy—a key goal for system development is to foster dynamic alignment between skills supply and demand. In hypothetical perfect markets, achieving this outcome would require little if any government action: individuals would recoup, through higher earnings, their investment of money and time to acquire skills; and firms likewise would obtain their returns from investing in worker training in the form of the increased productivity of their workforce. Yet hardly any country relies solely on such mechanisms to sustain a balance between skills supply and demand. More often market forces and government action must work together toward this objective, playing complementary roles to overcome impediments posed by imperfections in labor and capital markets, as well as failures in decision making (see Robalino, Almeida, and Behrman 2012 for a detailed discussion).[1]

From the perspective of policy makers with a practical agenda to improve the functioning WfD systems, it is important to go beyond abstract considerations about market and government failure. What is needed is to identify the main stakeholders in WfD, clarify their roles, and understand the institutional arrangements by which key functions in the system are discharged. For this task, the World Bank's Systems Approach for Better Education Results-Workforce Development (SABER-WfD) framework and tool, described more fully in World Bank (2013), provides a systematic approach for thinking about the issues and for targeted data collection and analysis. It focuses on the scope for action by the government to address market and government failures that contribute to suboptimal workforce development outcomes. It has this focus not because government has the most important role among stakeholders, but because government is a natural convener and facilitator of dialogue on institutional weaknesses and priorities for policy development and implementation.[2] The next section summarizes key features of the SABER-WfD framework and tool to provide context for the subsequent presentation of the data and findings based on their application in 27 countries and the West Bank and Gaza.[3]

The SABER-WfD Conceptual Framework

The demand for skills is not static. It evolves both with changes in demography and technology and in response to business practices and government policies. The SABER-WfD framework, illustrated in figure 3.1, recognizes that bringing the skills supply into dynamic alignment with demand is a central aim of WfD policies and institutions.[4] Such alignment improves the match between skills and jobs, which, in turn, helps to enhance the economic well-being of individuals, firms, and communities. Weak policies and institutions, on the other

Figure 3.1 SABER-WfD's Conceptual Framework for Dialogue on Workforce Development

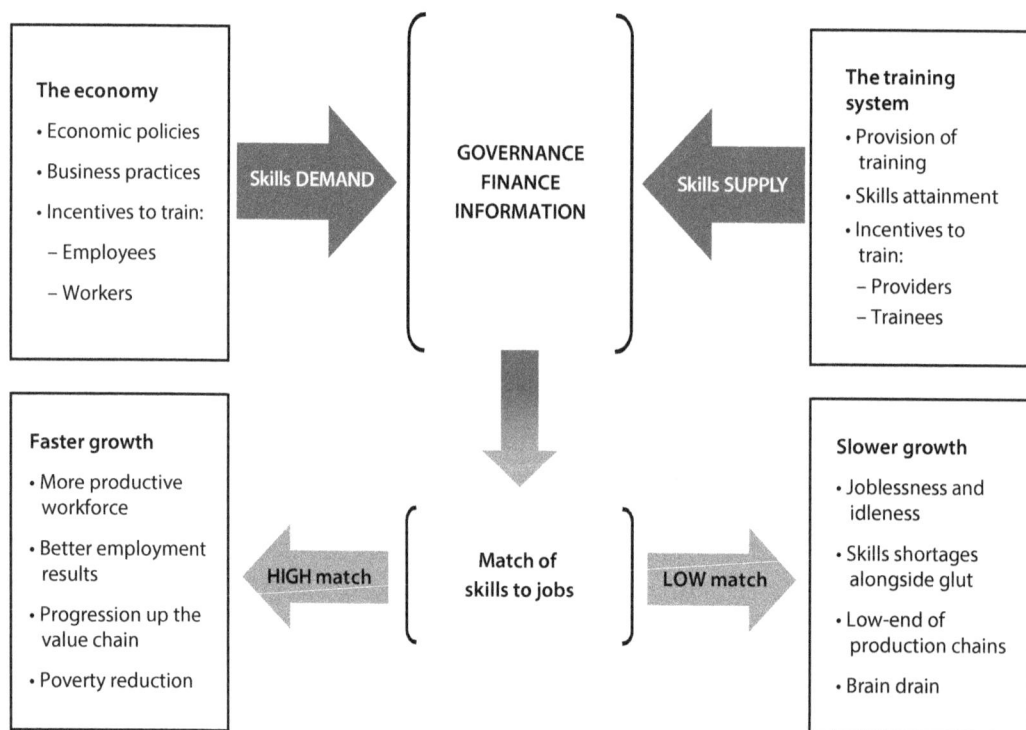

Source: Adapted from World Bank 2013.
Note: SABER = Systems Approach for Better Education Results; WfD = workforce development.

hand, drive a wedge between skills supply and demand, leading to wasted investments in skills, unfilled vacancies, and poor economic outcomes.

Misalignment between the skills supply and demand stems from many causes, among them market failures. To rationalize dialogue on how government intervention might best address the problems, the SABER-WfD framework focuses on three major areas that warrant attention: governance, finance, and information. These aspects of policy are connected to each other in the sense that governance arrangements define the architecture of the institutional structure through which resources, in the form of money and information, flow. These resources in turn influence the choices and actions of individuals, training providers, employers, and firms and therefore influence the performance of the system of workforce development.

The scope and importance of each of these areas may be summarized as follows:

- *Governance.* Workforce development concerns at least four sets of stakeholders: (1) national leaders and public officials from different ministries; (2) employers, individually and through their trade associations, as a source of jobs, market intelligence, expertise, and support; (3) training institutions, again individually and corporately, as providers of training- and career-related services and as sources of potential recruits for employers; and (4) individuals, first as trainees and then as participants in the labor force, whether in self-employment or working for others. Governance arrangements define the nature and quality of the relationships among the stakeholders by clarifying roles and responsibilities, by influencing the incentives for cooperation and coordination, and by shaping the various parties' accountability for results.
- *Finance.* All WfD systems require adequate and well-deployed resources, both financial and nonfinancial, to function effectively. How money is mobilized, allocated, and disbursed shapes incentives and therefore the decisions made by individuals, training providers, and employers and firms in their capacity as trainers and users of skills. Policy issues include budget amounts and their distribution, criteria for allocations and continuation of funding, diversity in the sources of funding for investments in workforce development, and the availability of options for individuals and employers to finance their investments in skills acquisition. Because funding arrangements affect both skills supply and demand, they are a powerful lever for bringing these two sides of the skills equation into alignment.
- *Information.* Decision making in workforce development also benefits from knowledge about the market for skills, such as the extent and nature of skills gaps and mismatches, the menu and quality of training options and their costs, the employment and earnings of graduates of VET programs, the trustworthiness of the certification of skills attained, and the pathways for continued learning and career development. The routine

collection and dissemination of such information to the key stakeholders—individuals, employers, and training providers—is another powerful lever at the government's disposal for improving the system's performance. A more proactive intervention beyond simply facilitating information flows may also be appropriate in some situations. For example, training providers may be unable or unwilling to offer the training required to deepen the technological capabilities of industry clusters prioritized in the country's growth strategy. If so, government action to coordinate and elicit the initial supply response can help ease the skills constraints faced by these clusters.

Features of the SABER-WfD Tool

To translate the SABER-WfD framework into a practical tool for analyzing countries' institutions and praxis relating to WfD, we focus on three functional dimensions of decision making by policy makers and other stakeholders: Strategic Framework, System Oversight, and Service Delivery (figure 3.2).[5] At each level, the actions of the relevant principals affect different aspects of governance, finance, and information flows relating to WfD and thus the alignment between skills supply and demand. Documenting and analyzing these actions and the institutional structures through which they are mediated is the purpose of the SABER-WfD tool. For the purpose at hand,

Figure 3.2 Three Functional Dimensions of Decision Making in the SABER-WfD Framework

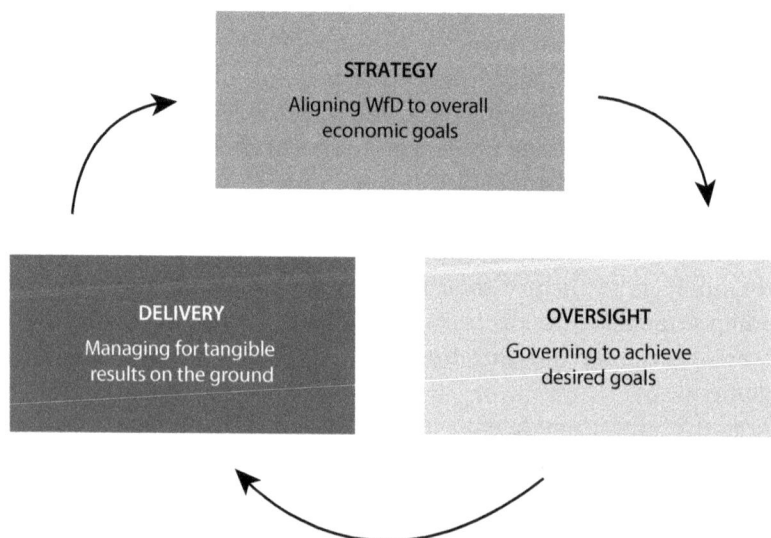

Source: World Bank 2013.
Note: SABER = Systems Approach for Better Education Results; WfD = workforce development.

the SABER-WfD tool relies on a structured questionnaire or data collection instrument and standardized protocols for data collection and analysis.[6]

To generate useful data, the SABER-WfD questionnaire is designed to elicit facts rather than opinions about a country's or a region's institutional arrangements for WfD and the praxis of policy making and implementation.[7] Its key features may be highlighted as follows:

- On *Strategic Framework*, the questionnaire documents the existence and nature of advocacy, partnership, and coordination, typically across traditional administrative boundaries, to advance the goal of aligning WfD to priorities for national development.
- On *System Oversight*, the questionnaire documents the arrangements and practices for funding, quality assurance, and learning pathways that influence choices by individuals, employers, and training providers to invest in skills formation.
- On *Service Delivery*, the questionnaire documents the diversity, organization, management, and operations of training provision, both state and nonstate. The data are intended to reveal the extent to which the system enables individuals to acquire market- and job-relevant skills.

To elaborate, the institutions and actions relating to Strategic Framework affect the WfD system as a whole and position it in relation to the rest of the economy, to the social context, and to the socioeconomic goals of the country or region. Therefore, the decision makers are high-level officials and stakeholders with influence over the system's overall orientation and trajectory; they are typically leaders with mandates above the sector ministries. They can thus decide on the priority of WfD in relation to other national agendas and remove or at least minimize structural obstacles that undermine the link between skills demand and supply.

With regard to System Oversight, the focus is on institutions and actions at the level of line ministries and the relevant nongovernment counterparts. These ministries and counterparts define the structures, rules, standards, benchmarks, and other "rules of the game" that guide the activities of the WfD system's main participants, specifically individuals, training institutions, and employers, whether in the public or in the private sector. The relevant line ministries are typically those overseeing education and labor but often also include those responsible for WfD activities targeting specific populations, such as youth or women. The relevant nongovernment counterparts are those with a systemic mandate, such as representatives of employer or worker groups.

Regarding Service Delivery, the SABER-WfD tool treats service providers as the relevant unit of analysis; the principal agents here are thus the managers of institutions or organizations—both public and private—that offer training or skills development services to individuals. The individuals who enter training may be enrolled on their own account, or they may be sent for training by their employers.[8]

Decision making at the three functional dimensions are clearly interrelated, although in reality the linkages may be weak or even absent altogether. Decisions pertaining to strategic framing create the authorizing environment for system oversight that, in turn, defines the context for the operations of individual training providers. The loop is closed when the results achieved by the service providers are used as feedback by decision makers at the strategic level to gauge the system's overall performance in supplying job-relevant skills and to guide reforms for improvement.

The SABER-WfD questionnaire, while intentionally parsimonious, contains sufficient detail to inform assessment of the depth of capacity in the WfD system to design, coordinate, implement, and learn from policy experience. As figure 3.3 indicates, the questions are grouped around nine substantive areas, three under each functional dimension.[9] Organizing the data in this way enables, within each dimension, a systematic investigation of any critical challenges in governance, finance, and information that might be undermining alignment between skills supply and demand.[10] This organization allows a detailed, structured narrative on system capacity to emerge from the qualitative data. Furthermore, by reducing

Figure 3.3 Functional Dimensions and Major Topics in the SABER-WfD Tool

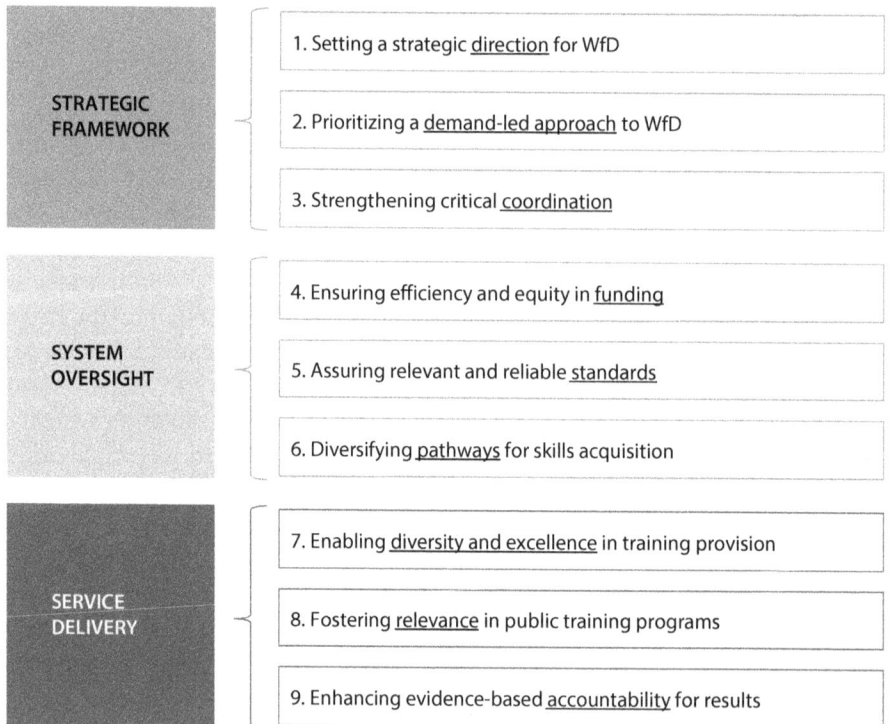

STRATEGIC FRAMEWORK
1. Setting a strategic <u>direction</u> for WfD
2. Prioritizing a <u>demand-led approach</u> to WfD
3. Strengthening critical <u>coordination</u>

SYSTEM OVERSIGHT
4. Ensuring efficiency and equity in <u>funding</u>
5. Assuring relevant and reliable <u>standards</u>
6. Diversifying <u>pathways</u> for skills acquisition

SERVICE DELIVERY
7. Enabling <u>diversity and excellence</u> in training provision
8. Fostering <u>relevance</u> in public training programs
9. Enhancing evidence-based <u>accountability</u> for results

Source: World Bank 2013.
Note: SABER = Systems Approach for Better Education Results; WfD = workforce development.

ambiguity in terminology and concepts, the approach creates common ground for policy exchange on a complex subject among inevitably heterogeneous interlocutors.

Notes

1. See appendix A for a brief summary of these issues and examples of government action to address information imperfections, a market failure that has received particular attention.

2. Thus the actions of individual employers and education and training institutions to provide education and training to students and workers are directly examined only insofar as they relate to formal workforce development policies and institutions (whether publicly or privately organized, administered, and funded). Although in many systems private actors provide a large portion of training in a manner that does not rely on public policy for coordination, the scope, quality, and relevance of these activities are not directly assessed under the SABER-WfD tool, because a variety of other initiatives already examine these issues in many partner countries.

3. The 27 countries include: Armenia, Bulgaria, Chile, the Arab Republic of Egypt, Georgia, Grenada, Iraq, Ireland, Jordan, the Republic of Korea, Lao People's Democratic Republic, the former Yugoslav Republic of Macedonia, Malaysia, Moldova, Morocco, Singapore, the Solomon Islands, Sri Lanka, St. Lucia, Tajikistan, Timor-Leste, Tunisia, Turkey, Uganda, Ukraine, Vietnam, and the Republic of Yemen. Among them, the following five had data for at least two years: Chile, Ireland, Korea, Malaysia, and Singapore.

4. See World Bank (2013) for a more detailed discussion of skills demand and supply.

5. The actions by policy makers affect both government and nongovernment stakeholders, either directly or indirectly through their influence on the environment in which these stakeholders operate.

6. The SABER-WfD questionnaire seeks to document the existence, content, and implementation of WfD policies and institutions for the system in question. Therefore, it is not completed in the same way as a survey questionnaire administered to individuals.

7. The SABER-WfD data collection instrument may be found at http://wbgfiles .worldbank.org/documents/hdn/ed/saber/supporting_doc/Background/WFD /Questionnaire_WfD.pdf.

8. Although all levels and types of education and training are relevant to WfD, the SABER-WfD framework and tool focus on activity that takes place after basic education, as explained in section 2 above.

9. To enhance comparability in the data across and within the three dimensions, the questions in each major area considered in the SABER-WfD tool share two generic features: (1) they take stock of the institutions and praxis pertaining to the area of interest; and (2) they examine the functioning of these institutions by posing questions about the existence and use of mechanisms for continuous improvement through monitoring, evaluation, learning, and adjustment.

10. The challenges in governance, finance, and information associated with the three functional dimensions considered in the SABER-WfD framework may not manifest themselves in the same way across the three dimensions.

References

Robalino, David, Rita Almeida, and Jere Behrman. 2012. "Policy Framework: The Economic Rationale for Skills Development Policies." In *The Right Skills for the Job? Rethinking Effective Training Policies for Workers*, edited by Rita Almeida, Jere Behrman, and David Robalino, 49–66. Washington, DC: Social Protection, Human Development Network, World Bank.

World Bank. 2013. "What Matters for Workforce Development: A Framework and Tool for Analysis." SABER Working Paper 6, World Bank, Washington, DC.

CHAPTER 4

Data and Highlights from the Application of the SABER-WfD Tool

The qualitative nature of the information sought by the Systems Approach for Better Education Results (SABER) questionnaire poses challenges for both data collection and analysis. This chapter explains the steps taken to address the main concerns and presents highlights from the data collected so far for 27 countries and the West Bank and Gaza.[1]

Data Collection, Validation, and Analysis

Data collection begins at the invitation of a participating country. Once agreement is reached to launch a SABER-WfD (Workforce Development) study, a principal investigator is hired to take charge of data collection and prepare a report based on the data collected. This investigator would be knowledgeable about the system for workforce development and would typically have contacts among the key players in the system. The mechanics for completing the questionnaire are simple: for each question, the principal investigator selects from a closed list of answer options and justifies the choice(s) with evidence from published reports or interviews with credible informants.[2] As desired, additional explanation or contextual information may be supplied, particularly as an aid for report writing later on. In practice, the qualitative nature of the exercise exposes it to ambiguities that can compromise data quality and consistency. The risk is managed by applying standard protocols to collect and validate the data.

To ensure that similar protocols are followed in data collection, each principal investigator receives systematic training combined with a mix of scheduled and ad hoc technical support.[3] The training is offered by the SABER-WfD technical team and consists of a four-module program covering all aspects of the work. The first two modules occur at the start of the principal investigator's work and provide orientation and guidance on compiling the evidence and using it to complete the SABER-WfD questionnaire. The third module takes place when the principal investigator has completed this assignment and submits the data for preliminary analysis by the SABER-WfD team. It explains the validation process that the principal investigator is expected to conduct with support from the World Bank task team leader and the SABER-WfD technical team. The main activity at this stage is a workshop to which participants representing the relevant state and nonstate agencies and stakeholders are invited. The meeting, which follows a standard agenda, convenes a group of well-informed stakeholders, state and non-state, to scrutinize the SABER-WfD data. The aim of the meeting is to solicit input to correct errors of fact or interpretation and thus enhance the complete-ness and accuracy of the data. Following this phase, the fourth module of training is offered to the principal investigator, mainly to guide the use of the data and the analytical results to prepare the SABER-WfD country report.[4]

By combining three elements—explicit guidelines, technical support, and expertise to scrutinize the data—the process produces data that are reasonably reliable and comparable across countries (or regions) even if it does not, and indeed cannot, eliminate all ambiguities. As part of a continuing effort to improve data quality and gain speed in data collection and validation, the protocols now feature a crowdsourcing arrangement (box 4.1) to streamline and intensify the mobilization of local knowledge for data collection and validation.

The answer options selected in response to the questions for each topic in the SABER-WfD questionnaire are scored on a four-point scale against predefined rubrics based on available knowledge on global good practice (see figure 4.1).[5] To improve consistency in applying the scoring rubrics, at least two persons on the World Bank's SABER-WfD team score the data as separate, parallel exercises. Often they award similar scores, but discrepancies are typically unavoidable given the qualitative nature of the data. Differences in scores are resolved by clarifying and adjusting the underlying evidence in consultation with the relevant principal investigator. A data validation workshop is held to convene knowledgeable

---

Box 4.1 Crowdsourcing SABER-WfD Data

Crowdsourcing is a method for participatory data collection aimed at improving its accuracy, completeness, and timeliness. It also helps foster dialogue among stakeholders who might otherwise have few opportunities for interaction on issues of a systemic nature, reinforcing existing processes for system management and reform. Crowdsourcing for SABER-WfD (Systems Approach for Better Education Results-Workforce Development) was first tested in the Solomon Islands, where SABER-WfD was used to inform the creation of an apex human resources coordinating committee. "Awareness is the major change," commented one partici-pating official. "The assessment informed our national consultation of what we missed and what we need to do, from looking at key policies and substance."

Components of the crowdsourcing model appear in figure B4.1.1. The research team first makes its best effort to fill the SABER-WfD questionnaire based on documentary evidence on hand, supplemented by interviews with a few selected informants. This initial work yields data

box continues next page

Box 4.1 Crowdsourcing SABER-WfD Data *(continued)*

Figure B4.1.1 Collecting SABER-WfD Data through Crowdsourcing

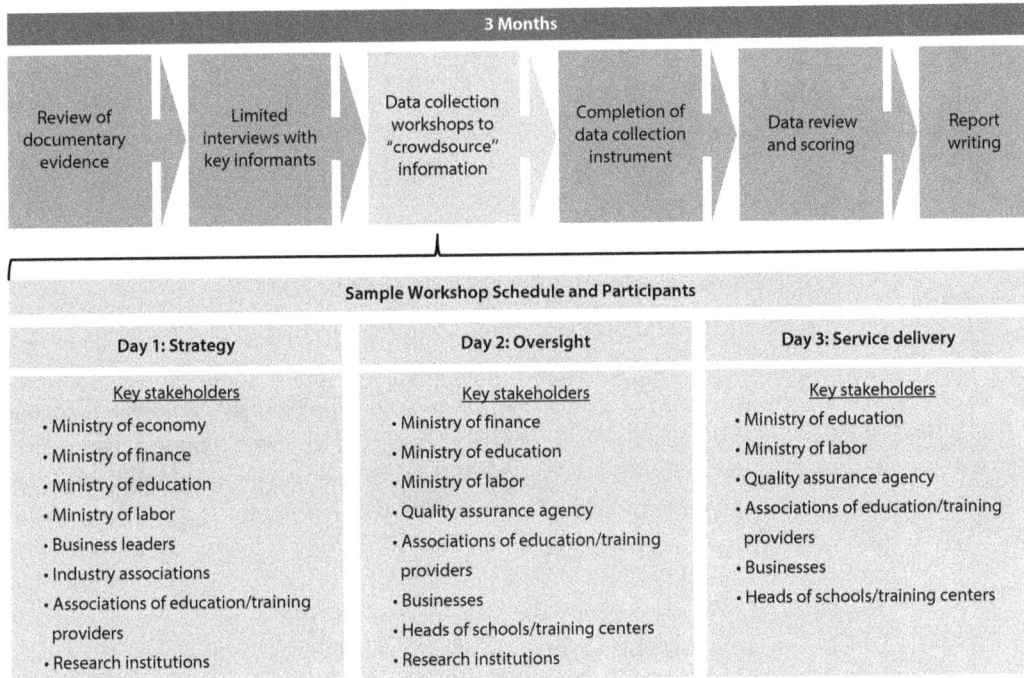

3 Months					
Review of documentary evidence	Limited interviews with key informants	Data collection workshops to "crowdsource" information	Completion of data collection instrument	Data review and scoring	Report writing

Sample Workshop Schedule and Participants

Day 1: Strategy	**Day 2: Oversight**	**Day 3: Service delivery**
Key stakeholders	Key stakeholders	Key stakeholders
• Ministry of economy • Ministry of finance • Ministry of education • Ministry of labor • Business leaders • Industry associations • Associations of education/training providers • Research institutions	• Ministry of finance • Ministry of education • Ministry of labor • Quality assurance agency • Associations of education/training providers • Businesses • Heads of schools/training centers • Research institutions	• Ministry of education • Ministry of labor • Quality assurance agency • Associations of education/training providers • Businesses • Heads of schools/training centers

Source: World Bank construction.
Note: SABER = Systems Approach for Better Education Results; WfD = Workforce Development.

for completing a preliminary version of the questionnaire, provides the basis for computing preliminary SABER-WfD scores, and helps in identifying invitees to a workshop to discuss the tentative results. Through a facilitated dialogue the invited stakeholders—who are grouped based on their area of expertise—validate the information or correct it, supply insights to aid interpretation of the data, and fill information gaps where needed. The process seeks consensus on the appropriate choice of responses to questions in the SABER-WfD questionnaire. Once the data are reviewed and confirmed, they are rescored to obtain the SABER-WfD scores that form the basis for the country-specific SABER-WfD reports posted at http://saber .worldbank.org/index.cfm.

stakeholders in the country (government and nongovernment) to confirm the accuracy and completeness of data collection. Based on feedback from the workshop, the principal investigator reviews and updates the questionnaire as needed. Adjusted areas of the questionnaire are reviewed and rescored by the SABER-WfD team. The finalized topic scores are consolidated using simple averages to obtain the corresponding scores at the subsequent levels of aggregation and at the level of policy actions, goals, and dimensions.[6]

Figure 4.1 SABER-WfD Scoring Rubrics

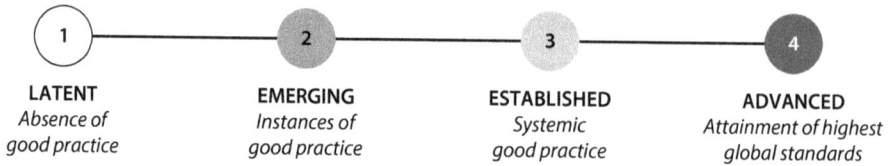

1	2	3	4
LATENT	**EMERGING**	**ESTABLISHED**	**ADVANCED**
Absence of good practice	*Instances of good practice*	*Systemic good practice*	*Attainment of highest global standards*

Source: World Bank 2013.
Note: SABER = Systems Approach for Better Education Results; WfD = Workforce Development.

Pattern in Dimension-Level Scores across Countries

Following the scoring procedure, data were gathered and analyzed for 27 countries. An initial version of the questionnaire was used in six pilot countries (Chile, Ireland, the Republic of Korea, Singapore, Uganda, Vietnam) and the Xinjiang Uygher Autonomous Region, China). Experience from these economies informed refinements to the SABER-WfD questionnaire.[7] The revised questionnaire (version 2.5) was then used for data collection in the other countries. For four of the pilot countries—Chile, Ireland, Korea, and Singapore—data were collected for multiple years to document their well-known histories of progress in workforce development. For the others, the data pertain to the most recent period for which data were available at the time of data collection, typically circa 2012. The only exception was Malaysia, for which data were collected, at the government's request, for two years, 2000 and 2010. In all of the economies, the questionnaire was completed using documentary evidence and information supplied by credible informants and was subsequently validated by knowledgeable reviewers, including government and nongovernment stakeholders and researchers. The overall pattern in the dimension-level SABER-WfD scores appears in figure 4.2.[8] Three features are noteworthy: (1) the positive relation between GDP (gross domestic product) per capita and dimension-level SABER-WfD scores; (2) the prevalence of higher scores at the Strategy Dimension in most systems dimensions, particularly those that perform well; and (3) the lack of patterns among dimension-level scores of low-performing systems where Strategy does not dominate consistently.

On the first point, dimension-level SABER-WfD scores rise with GDP per capita. This positive relationship characterizes all three dimensions in the SABER-WfD framework. It coheres with expectations about institutional culture and practices in richer countries: the leadership for WfD is broadened, depersonalized, and geared toward strategic goals; the analytical basis for policy development is strengthened; the financing for WfD is stabilized, diversified, and sensitive to the achievement of results; the pathways and standards for skill acquisition are formalized and enforced; the reliance on monitoring and evaluation and the sharing of information are made routine; the practice of continuous adjustments in light of changing circumstances is institutionalized, and so on. Nevertheless, there remains considerable variation around the regression lines,

Figure 4.2 Relation between Dimension-Level SABER-WfD Scores and GDP per capita, circa 2012

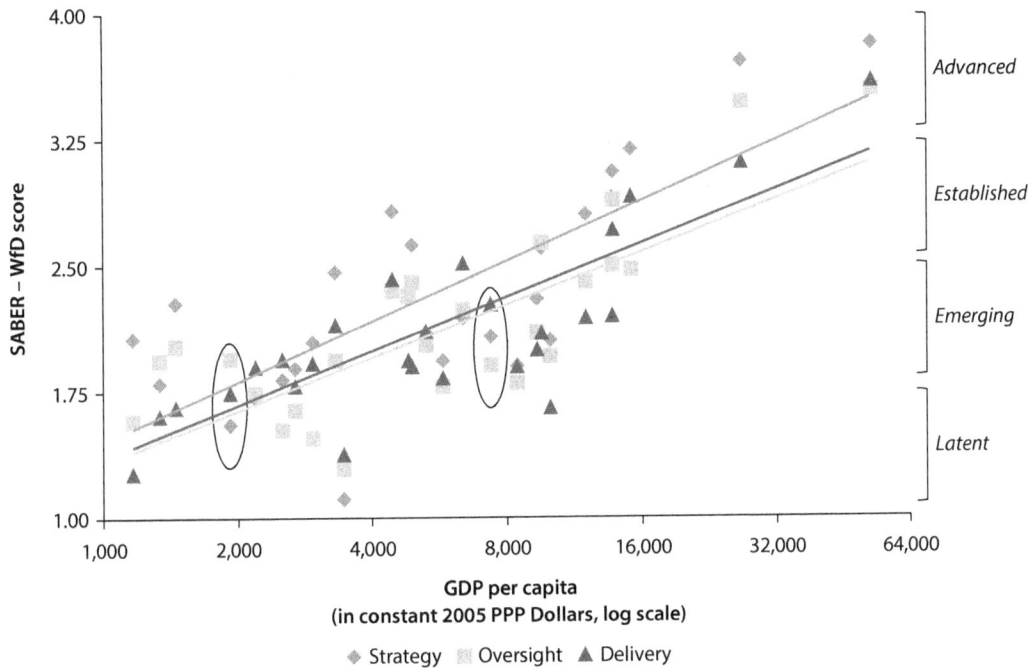

Source: World Bank construction based on SABER-WfD scores circa 2012 for 27 countries and the West Bank and Gaza.
Note: GDP = gross domestic product; PPP = purchasing power parity; SABER = Systems Approach for Better Education Results; WfD = Workforce Development.
Scoring: The scores reported in figure 4.2 are based on the raw scores for the 47 topics considered in the SABER-WfD questionnaire. Each topic is scored following protocols involving at least two independent scorers based on the SABER-WfD scoring rubric, which determines whether the system is Latent, Emerging, Established, or Advanced relative to global good practices. Standardized z-scores have also been calculated by subtracting the sample mean and dividing by the sample standard deviation for each dimension. Figure A1 shows their relation to GDP per capita.
Regression estimations: The colored lines in figure 4.2 show estimated regressions based on a generic specification of the following form: SABER-WfD score = $\alpha + \beta$ ln (GDP per capita). The estimated value of α for the regression for Strategy, Oversight, and Delivery are, respectively, 2.10, 1.82, 1.79; the corresponding values of β are 0.51, 0.46, and 0.45. The R^2 statistic for these regressions are, respectively, 0.58, 0.61, and 0.65.
Circled data points: For illustration, the two ovals encircle data for Tajikistan (on the left) and Armenia (on the right), countries with low-performing systems where the top score is for a SABER-WfD dimension other than Strategy.

suggesting that progress toward strong systemic arrangements is not entirely dependent on a country's material wealth.

Second, scores for Strategy generally dominate those for the other two functional dimensions. This pattern is evident from the location of the regression line for the Strategy dimension in figure 4.2 compared with those for Oversight and Service Delivery. The hierarchy is intuitive: by their nature, the actions associated with Strategy involve fewer agents and tend to require fewer steps to go from idea to implementation. Therefore, moving from a low score to a higher score for Strategy is more easily accomplished than would be the case for Oversight or Service Delivery. Improving scores for Oversight and Service Delivery almost always requires the cooperation of and contribution of information and effort from more and more stakeholders with highly diverse interests and priorities. This fact alone implies a more labor-intensive and time-consuming process to agree on action plans and the arrangements for implementation. For example, setting up a well-functioning qualifications framework—one aspect of Oversight in the SABER-WfD framework—calls for inputs from employers, curriculum experts, training providers, and skills assessors and requires agreement on standards and procedures for the assessment and certification of skills acquisition.

Third, in low-performing systems, the scores for Strategy no longer dominate consistently. For our purpose, such systems are those with no score across the three functional dimensions above the Emerging level. Of the 18 countries in this group, the score is highest for Strategy in only eight of them. In the remaining countries, the top score is attached either to Oversight, as in the Lao People's Democratic Republic, the West Bank and Gaza, and Tajikistan, or to Delivery, as in Armenia and Ukraine.[9] The significance of a lagging score for Strategy should not be overemphasized, but it may undermine efforts to improve Oversight and Delivery. For example, in the absence of strategic leadership, the legislative foundation for creating and sustaining the institutional infrastructure and mechanisms associated with these two functional dimensions of the WfD system may be weak or nonexistent. The result is to compromise the system's functional efficacy and efficiency. The experience of countries for which data covering multiple years are available is consistent with this understanding of the key role of Strategy in facilitating progress in institutional development and praxis in the Oversight and Delivery dimensions of WfD systems.

Scores of Countries with Multiyear Data

Data for multiple years were collected for Chile, Ireland, Korea, Malaysia, and Singapore. For Korea and Singapore the selected years—1970, 1990, and 2010— span a period of clear transition from emerging-economy status to high-income status. Workforce development had been an explicit and important component of Korea's and Singapore's economic strategy, and the selected years were chosen to track the evolution of institutional structure and praxis in the three functional dimensions addressed in the SABER-WfD framework. For Chile and Malaysia, two countries that also experienced economic development, the data cover only the last decade, the shorter period reflecting the paucity of documentary evidence and therefore the difficulty of assembling the desired information for earlier years. Finally, for Ireland, the data pertain to three years—1980, 1990, and 2000—covering a period of rapid economic transition during which WfD received significant attention as part of the government's economic growth strategy. The collapse of the Irish economy in the 2007 global financial crisis and its aftermath add a layer of complexity that would have detracted from our study's focus on the evolution of WfD institutions and praxis; to keep the analysis simple, particularly at this nascent stage of the SABER-WfD project, it was decided to collect data for Ireland only for the earlier years.

The time-series scores at the dimension level for the five countries appear in figure 4.3. By 2012 none of these countries had a low-performing WfD system, that is, a system with no dimension rated below the Established level.

Figure 4.3 Dimension-Level SABER-WfD Scores in Five Countries, 1970–circa 2010

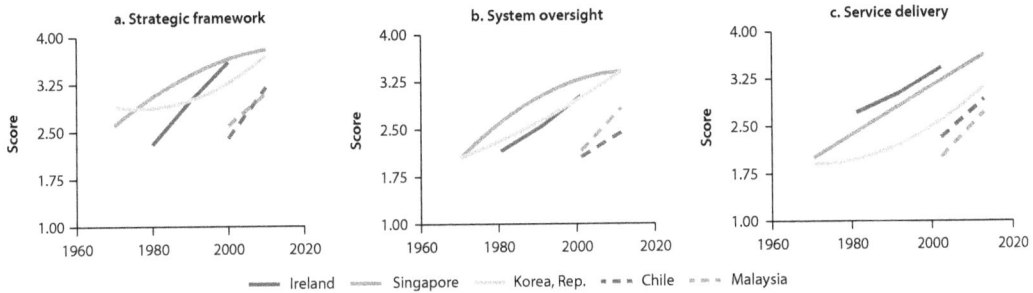

Source: World Bank analysis based on data collected using the SABER-WfD instrument.
Note: SABER = Systems Approach for Better Education Results; WfD = Workforce Development. For Chile the data refer to 2000 and 2011; for Malaysia, to 2000 and 2010; for Ireland, to 1980, 1990, and 2000; and for Singapore and Korea to 1970, 1990, and 2010.

Strategy almost always tops the scores or rises to that position with a lag. Indeed, it maintains its top position in four of the five countries throughout the periods covered. The exception is Ireland, where the score for Delivery in 1980 exceeded that for Strategy, a ranking that was reversed by 2000. This reversal coincides with the proactive stance taken by the Irish government in the 1990s in positioning WfD to support the country's businesses in the prioritized economic sectors, including information technology and pharmaceuticals (Hill, Hoffman, and Hoffman 2005). One aspect of this proactivity is the creation of new entities, notably the National Competitiveness Council, to provide coherent and well-informed leadership in connecting the WfD agenda to the country's economic priorities. Another is the expansion of the system of Institutes of Technology, a new type of tertiary-level institution that offers programs with a more practical—and more business-responsive—focus than the more academic offerings of the universities.

No score stagnates, but raising a score to the next level of performance does take time. In each of the five countries, the scores for Strategy, Oversight, and Delivery all register improvements in the time frame for which data are available, often with gains sufficient to reach the next level of performance along the four-point scale of Latent, Emerging, Established, and Advanced. The WfD systems of these countries benefit from systemic improvements in the institutions for and praxis of shaping policies as well as those for governing the functioning of the WfD system. These countries have taken a holistic approach to develop their WfD systems and have sustained the effort over long periods. Raising the score for Strategy from the Established to the Advanced level took Singapore about two decades; raising the score for Oversight from Emerging to Established also took Korea about two decades; and raising the score for Delivery from Emerging to Established took both Chile and Malaysia about a decade.

Scores improve along diverse trajectories, reflecting the likely influence of country conditions. That countries take different paths to stronger WfD systems is consistent with the fact that country conditions constrain as well as create space for reform. Chile and Malaysia share similar gains in the scores for Strategy and Delivery, but Malaysia has made more progress in raising its score for Oversight. One possible reason is that the country's more centralized form of government facilitated rapid introduction and successful implementation of the Malaysia Qualifications Framework. Chile also initiated reforms to strengthen its qualifications framework, notably through the Chile Califica (Chile Qualifies Program), but given its more decentralized and market-driven form of government, it appears that more time is needed to build consensus among employers for the creation and implementation of a single qualifications framework with wide scope and support.

Selected Comparisons of Country Experiences over Time

Singapore and Korea took different paths to high performance over four decades. Korea's scores for Strategy and Oversight caught up with those of Singapore after a lag, but its score for Delivery still lagged behind Singapore's in 2010, perhaps reflecting differences in economic strategy.[10] Singapore's strategy has relied heavily on foreign direct investments since the 1970s, an approach that necessitates productive engagement with a great variety and number of stakeholders, a more explicit specification of oversight arrangements, and a diversity of agile service providers that can respond quickly to market signals—all features that are rewarded in the SABER-WfD scoring rubrics. In contrast, Korea's economic strategy involved favoring large conglomerates that are central to driving the country's industrialization. The importance of these conglomerates and their focus in the early years on key industries, such as chemicals and heavy industries, exerted an important influence on Korea's approach to WfD. Engagement with employers focused mainly on the key players; oversight functions were geared to the needs of the prioritized industries; and diversity in service provision was neither needed nor encouraged. As the economy evolved, these features were replaced by those associated with more advanced systems, as the rising scores across all functional dimensions attest. Yet, the legacy of a highly centralized system of service delivery persists, which explains why Korea's score for Delivery in 2010 has not quite reached the Advanced level.

Malaysia and Korea exemplify different approaches to building a qualifications framework. In both countries, the rising scores for the Oversight dimension reflect, among other developments, improvements in the arrangements for quality assurance, building up from modest efforts initially.[11] A national qualifications framework is a popular instrument for this purpose, but as of this writing, Korea has yet to establish one, and Malaysia's was put in place only in 2007.[12]

Instead of a national qualifications framework, Korea emphasizes the concept of "transferable" skills and relies on several instruments for benchmarking skills to labor market needs, including the Korean National Competency Standards (KNCS) and the Korean Collegiate Essential Skills Assessment (K-CESA) (Jin 2014).[13] The KNCS started modestly. In 1968 competency standards were specified for just 15 occupations, based on standards used in the United Kingdom and Australia. Subsequent developments built on this modest start, including passage of the National Technical Qualifications Act in 1973, which laid the foundation for a national testing system based on standardized criteria and stakeholder input; consolidation in 2002 of various agencies' disparate efforts to define standards under a single authority charged with overseeing testing and certification; and a widening of the scope of competency standards covering a cumulative total of 250 occupations by 2010, most of them in Korea's priority economic sectors such as electronics, information and communication technology, and environmental engineering. The system today has robust arrangements for skills testing and certification, for engaging relevant stakeholders in curriculum development and revision to keep in step with evolving economic conditions, and for disseminating information to the public about skills standards and qualifications. Building on its current system of competency standards, Korea is now in the midst of creating a partial qualifications framework for vocational education and training (VET) and university engineering programs, which it expects to implement in 2017.

Malaysia's rising score in the Oversight dimension also signals, in part, a maturation of the arrangements for quality assurance, in this case in the form of a functioning, comprehensive national qualifications framework that engages the participation and support of employers. It built on the National Occupational Skills Standards (NOSS), set up in 1993, the same year the Human Resources Development Fund was established. The purpose of the fund was to provide training, retraining, and development of Malaysia's workforce to meet the demands of a knowledge-based high-income economy. The fund collects a mandatory levy from firms, which accumulates in firm-specific accounts from which employers can seek reimbursement for part of the costs incurred in providing training for their workers. The arrangement aligned incentives toward competency-based standards for training for employers and the government. Employers who outsourced their training needed an easy way to identify quality programs, and the government needed to ensure that the training that employers provided in-house (and against which they were claiming reimbursement from the fund) indeed met minimum standards of quality. New legislation in 1996—the Education Act, the Private Higher Educational Institutions Act, and the National Accreditation Board Act—expanded the application of state-mandated standards to providers of tertiary-level services. Nevertheless, the system remained fragmentary and lacked consistent input from industry and other nonstate actors.[14] The National Skills Development Act 2006 and the Malaysian Qualifications Agency Act 2007 ushered in significant improvements. The 2006 act required engagement with industry in the formulation of NOSS, and the 2007 act enabled the consolidation of a jumble of standards under the Malaysia Qualifications Framework, a broadening of the coverage of NOSS— reaching 1,585 occupations by 2010, up from just 467 in 2000—and a deepening in the range of skills levels.

Ireland and Chile have successfully fostered coordination between businesses and governments for both Strategy and Service Delivery. This success is reflected in the Advanced scores for strengthening strategic coordination and fostering relevance of training programs for both countries in the most recent study year. Their experiences show that either party can lead in establishing such coordination. In Chile, mining companies under the leadership of the Chilean Mining Council and in collaboration with suppliers and contractors, training providers, and the government created a two-pronged sector strategy for VET to ensure that it served their training needs (Innovum Fundación Chile n.d.). The first component, the Mining Skills Council (CCM), was financed entirely by participating mining firms and was created to modernize training in the sector and ensure its relevance through the development of a sectoral qualifications framework, creation of training packages, accreditation of programs, and research to identify skills gaps. The second component, called VetaMinera, sought to plug immediate skills gaps by serving in an intermediary role to provide information on occupations in mining to students, maintain a database of graduates in the sector, and provide a coordinating function to promote the use of industry-developed standards in training. Based on industry-provided information on training gaps, government funds (totaling almost two-thirds of total VetaMinera funding for the initial 2012–15 program duration) were made available to training providers on a competitive basis to encourage delivery of programs to address industry-identified gaps.

In Ireland, the government created the Skillsnets Training Network Program to use the National Training Fund (sustained through a levy of employee wages) to overcome coordination and financial barriers to firm-based training while increasing employer funds devoted to workforce up-skilling and re-skilling. Firms with similar training needs, often in a related industry or region, self select into networks and apply for funding through Skillsnets. Network member companies are able to purchase any type of training delivered through either classroom, on-the-job, or distance learning on a cost-matched basis using Skillsnet funds, while there are provisions for nonnetwork companies to participate at higher rates and limited state-subsidized places for unemployed individuals. The program has enjoyed success since inception, currently sustaining 62 training networks with total government contributions of €16 million.

Notes

1. Except for the five countries in the pilot cohort, data collection in each country was launched at the request of the relevant World Bank task team leader in the context of dialogue with his or her counterparts in government. For the pilot cohort, the work was launched by the SABER-WfD technical team.
2. Each country report based on the data collected lists the informants and their credentials.
3. The SABER-WfD technical team, based in Washington, DC, provides the training through video conferencing. The scheduled technical support takes place through

phone calls in the form of work-in-progress seminars with standard agenda appropriate to the particular stage of the work. Ad hoc support is arranged, as needed, to address issues on which a principal investigator may require additional clarification.

4. On occasion, inconsistences are uncovered during report writing, and in such instances, the underlying data are reviewed once more to resolve the remaining issues; completed reports are formally reviewed to meet quality standards before they are posted on the SABER website at http://saber.worldbank.org/index.cfm.

5. See World Bank (2013) for the rubrics used to score the SABER-WfD data.

6. Because composite scores are averages of the underlying scores at the topic level, they are rarely whole numbers. For presentation purposes, a composite score, X, may sometimes be shown as a categorical score based on the following conversion rule: $1.00 \leq X \leq 1.75$ converts to "Latent"; $1.75 < X \leq 2.50$ to "Emerging"; $2.50 < X \leq 3.25$ to "Established"; and $3.25 < X \leq 4.00$ to "Advanced."

7. Changes were made to improve the precision of the questions and their answer options, to reduce repetition, and to rationalize the way the questions were grouped and sequenced.

8. As explained, because the scores at the dimension level are averages of the underlying scores, they are typically not whole numbers that correspond precisely to the four-point scoring rubric indicated in figure 4.2.

9. To avoid cluttering the figure, only the data for two countries, Armenia and Tajikistan, are circled for illustrative purposes.

10. SABER-WfD reports for these countries are posted at http://saber.worldbank.org /index.cfm.

11. Unless otherwise indicated, the details about these two countries can be found in the country-specific SABER-WfD reports posted at the SABER website at http://saber .worldbank.org/index.cfm.

12. In 2015 more than 150 countries (among the 193 sovereign states recognized by the United Nations) have a national qualifications framework (NQF), up from a mere handful before 2000; the addition of new countries being concentrated during 2008–12 (UILL, ETF, and Cedefop 2015). Significant diversity exists across countries in how well the frameworks function and in their scope, which ranges from comprehensive coverage of all types and levels of qualification to limited coverage of only vocational education and training.

13. The Career Development Competency (CDC) instrument focuses on career planning and preparation.

14. One system, the National Accreditation Board (Lembaga Akreditasi Nasional), covered only tertiary-level private sector institutions; the other system, National Occupational Skills Standards (NOSS) covered only public skills training programs.

References

Hill, Kent, Dennis Hoffman, and Mary K. Hoffman. 2005. *Lessons from the "Irish Miracle."* Tempe, AZ: W. P. Carey School of Business, Arizona State University.

Innovum Fundación Chile (IFC). n.d. *Chilean Large-Scale Mining Workforce 2014–2023. Results and Conclusions.* Santiago, Chile: Consejo Minero.

Jin, Mi-Sug. 2014. "Transferable Skills Education in Technical and Vocational Education and Training (TVET) in the Republic of Korea." Sejong-si: Korea Research Institute of Vocational Education and Training. http://www.tvet-online.asia/issue3/jin_tvet3.pdf.

UILL (UNESCO Institute of Lifelong Learning), European Training Foundation (ETF), and European Centre for the Development of Vocational Training (Cedefop). 2015. *Global Inventory of Regional and National Qualifications Frameworks*, Vol. 1. (Prepublication copy issued for the ASEM Ministers of Education Meeting, Riga, April 2015.) Hamburg: UNESCO Institute of Lifelong Learning.

CHAPTER 5

Underpinnings of the Dimension-Level SABER-WfD Scores

The dimension-level scores are composites of the more detailed ratings of institutions, policies, and practices that affect a workforce development (WfD) system's coherence and capabilities. This chapter elaborates on these functions in the 22 countries for which comparable data are available as of this writing.[1] For each aspect considered, the data are presented as simple counts of the sample countries across the Latent, Emerging, Established, and Advanced categories. The presentation draws attention to common pressure points and areas of diversity in system performance across countries; as such, it highlights priorities for dialogue, learning, and attention in policy development. Following a brief summary of the dimension-level scores, the discussion in subsequent sections drills down on each dimension to reveal details about the underlying drivers of performance.

In figure 5.1 panels a, b, and c show three icons designed to help readers navigate the 13 graphs in this chapter that present the detailed Systems Approach for Better Education Results-Workforce Development (SABER-WfD) findings. In each graph, one of these icons appears at the top left corner to indicate the link between the findings shown and the three-level analytical structure of the SABER-WfD tool of dimensions, policy goals, and policy actions, as explained in chapter 3. Graphs with an icon that has all of its left-hand tiles colored (as in panel a) present dimension-level findings. When just one tile and all three bars beside it are colored (b), the findings drill down to the policy goal level within the indicated dimension. When the icon shows only a single bar in color (c), the findings drill down to the policy action level within the indicated policy goal.

Distribution of Countries by Dimension-Level Scores

The sample countries cluster in the Emerging category for all three dimensions, and none performs at the Advanced level in any dimension (figure 5.2). Differences are nonetheless discernible: countries score better on Strategic Framework than

Figure 5.1 Navigating the Presentation of the SABER-WfD Scores and Their Underpinnings

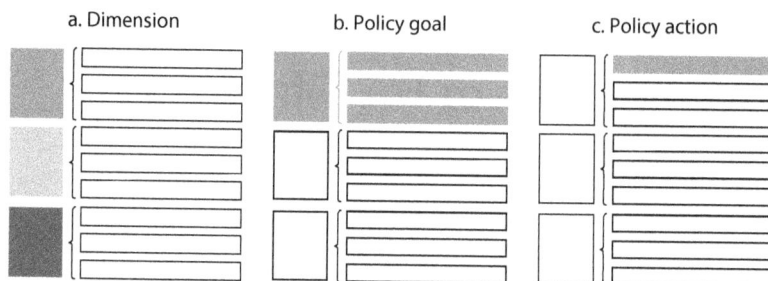

a. Dimension   b. Policy goal   c. Policy action

Figure 5.2 Distribution of Dimension-Level Scores

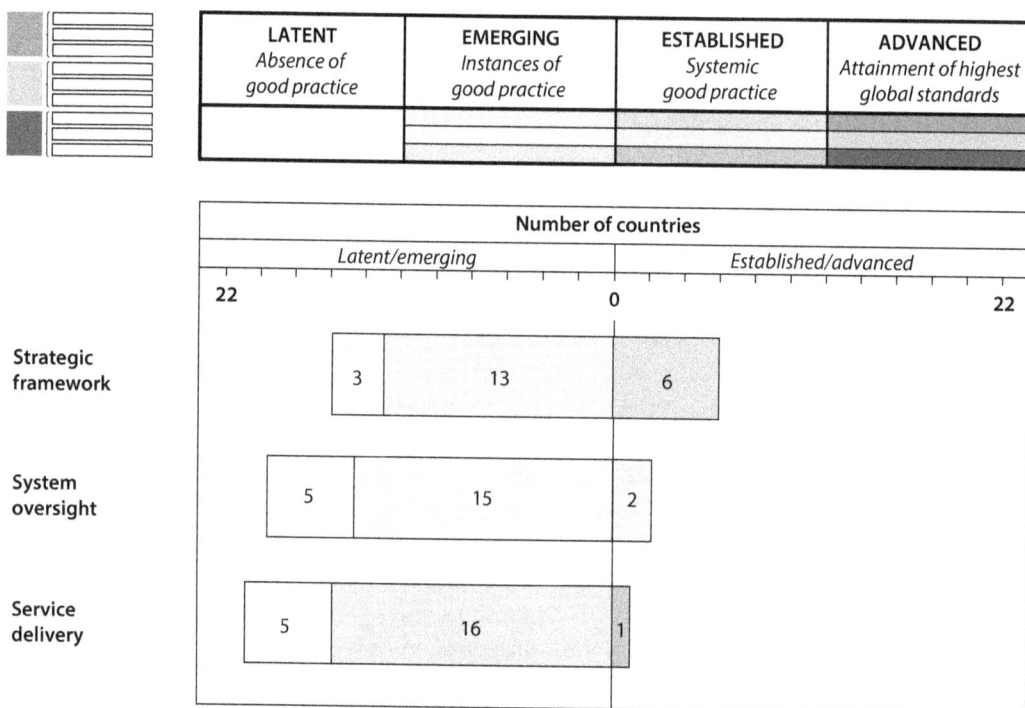

LATENT	EMERGING	ESTABLISHED	ADVANCED
Absence of good practice	Instances of good practice	Systemic good practice	Attainment of highest global standards

Source: World Bank construction based on data for 22 countries that were collected between 2011 and 2014 when the current version of the SABER-WfD (Systems Approach for Better Education Results-Workforce Development) questionnaire was introduced on a rolling basis as countries joined the program.

on System Oversight or Service Delivery, a pattern consistent with that in multi-year data presented in chapter 4. Among the six countries with an Established score for Strategic Framework, only two, Malaysia and Grenada, score at the Established level for System Oversight, and for Service Delivery only Malaysia achieves this level of performance. Noteworthy from figure 5.2 are the 13 Latent scores across the three dimensions; they belong to nine countries, which represent some 40 percent of our sample; the prevalence of low scores suggests that WfD systems are indeed nascent in many of the countries studied.[2]

Strategic Framework and Its Underpinnings

The dimension score is a summary reading of (in this case) the quality of leadership to align a country's WfD strategy and the system's development with its broader goals for economic growth, employment, and poverty reduction. Three factors receive explicit consideration in the SABER-WfD tool: (1) the inclusiveness of and confidence in the country's Strategic Direction for WfD strategy; (2) the robustness of Strategic Partnership between the government and key stakeholders, particularly employers; and (3) the tangibility of Strategic Coordination of effort to implement key WfD initiatives at the leadership level. Before probing into the content of these abbreviated descriptors, consider the patterns in figure 5.3.

The sample countries have more difficulty forming and sustaining strategic partnerships with employers than with articulating a direction for WfD or ensuring coordination of effort on specific priorities. Just three countries in figure 5.3 are rated Established or better on Partnership, compared with six and eight, respectively, for the other two areas. Conversely, 19 countries fall into the bottom

Figure 5.3 Strategic Framework and Its Underpinnings

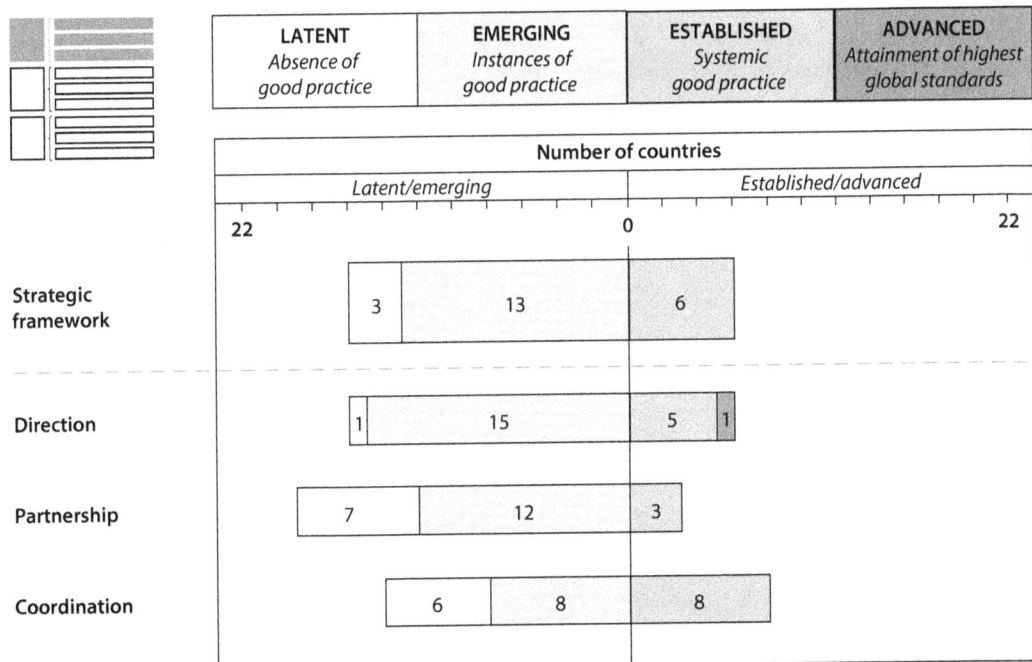

LATENT *Absence of good practice*	EMERGING *Instances of good practice*	ESTABLISHED *Systemic good practice*	ADVANCED *Attainment of highest global standards*

Number of countries

	Latent/emerging		Established/advanced	
	22	0		22
Strategic framework	3	13	6	
Direction	1	15	5	1
Partnership	7	12	3	
Coordination	6	8	8	

Source: World Bank construction based on data for 22 countries.

Workforce Development in Emerging Economies • http://dx.doi.org/10.1596/978-1-4648-0850-0

half of the scale (of which seven are in the Latent group) on Partnership, compared with 16 and 14, respectively, for the other two areas.

A more nuanced view follows on each of the three subdimension components—Strategic Direction, Partnership, and Coordination.

Strategic Direction

Two factors influence the score for Strategic Direction: (1) the *quality and scope of high-level advocacy* by champions that elevate WfD concerns to national prominence; and (2) the *substantive content of advocacy* by such champions.[3] Figure 5.4 shows the distribution of countries along these aspects of their WfD systems.

Countries in the sample are better at conceptualizing WfD strategy than at finding high-level government and nongovernment leaders to articulate and support the strategy through sustained public advocacy. Of the 22 countries in the sample, 16 score no higher than Emerging on the quality and scope of high-level advocacy by leaders implying that in many countries, advocacy for WfD generally proceeds on an ad hoc basis. By contrast, 14 countries are in the Established group for the substantive content of high-level advocacy, and one country, Malaysia, is even rated at the Advanced level. These patterns are consistent with the possibility that conceptualizing strategy, often an exercise performed by technical staff, materializes more easily than advocacy, which requires its practitioners to own the message and expend political capital to build consensus that is broad-based and effective in catalyzing action. In other words, although countries may have the

Figure 5.4 Strategic Direction and the Underlying Drivers

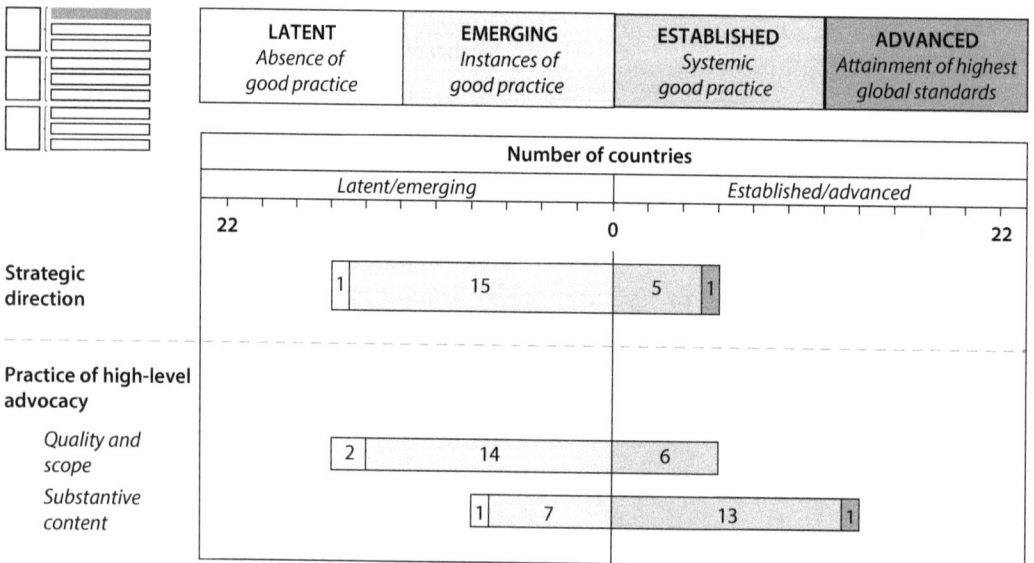

Source: World Bank construction based on data for 22 countries.

technical know-how to formulate strategy, the leadership necessary to sustain implementation for results often lags behind.

Strategic Partnership

The score on Strategic Partnership considers the following drivers of performance: (1) the availability of credible *assessments of skills needs* and gaps as a basis for informed collaboration among stakeholders; and (2) the quality of *engagement with employers*.[4] The results are shown in figure 5.5.

The sample countries are somewhat better at establishing, through credible skills assessments, an informed basis for collaboration among stakeholders than they are at forging effective engagement with employers, with the use of financial incentives being an area of particular weakness. On assessment of skills demand, the distribution of countries is similar for both economy-wide assessments and for focused analysis of the conditions in priority economic sectors. With regard to employer engagement, the scores for outreach (that is, involvement of employers in formulating strategy and developing policy) are diverse, with the sample countries' ratings spread evenly from Latent to Established. By contrast, employer engagement in the form of incentives for workforce training— offering financial incentives and monitoring them for impact—is rare, with the

Figure 5.5 Strategic Partnership and the Underlying Drivers

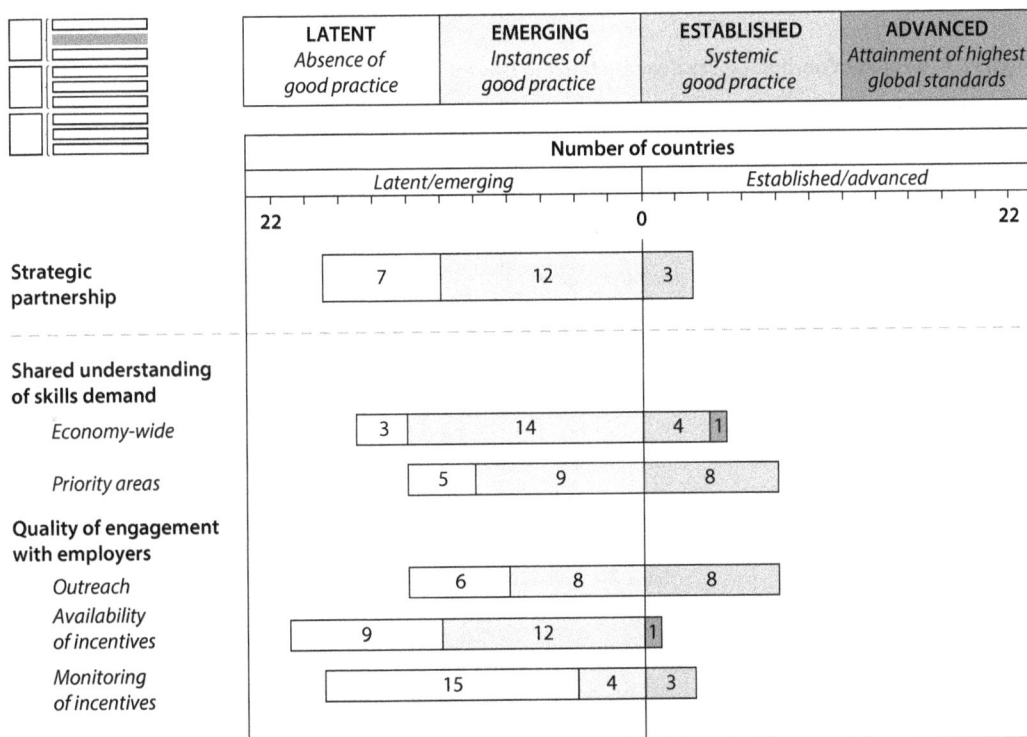

Source: World Bank construction based on data for 22 countries.

majority of countries falling in the Latent or Emerging categories. The one Advanced score for incentives belongs to Malaysia, which has put in place a Human Resources Development Fund (HRDF) to which employers may apply for partial reimbursement of employee training.[5]

Strategic Coordination

The focus here is on the capacity for effective coordination of effort at the leadership level to achieve tangible progress on WfD priorities. Two factors drive the score in the SABER-WfD assessment: (1) the organizational and governance structures that specify and formalize *roles and responsibilities in WfD* in government and nongovernment entities; and (2) evidence of *action on WfD priorities* that enjoy broad ownership at the leadership level, which is an indicator of the extent to which the WfD system enables coordinated action when there is agreement on strategic priorities. The assumption is that coordination is easier when there is broad ownership of a priority, so measure provides best case estimate of the capacity of the system for coordinated action. Figure 5.6 shows the distribution of countries by scoring category in these two areas.

The roles and responsibilities for WfD are generally clearer for government stakeholders than nongovernment stakeholders in the sample countries. Although every country in the sample has taken steps to define, to varying degrees of clarity, the functions of government stakeholders, four of these countries lacked even

Figure 5.6 Strategic Coordination and the Underlying Drivers

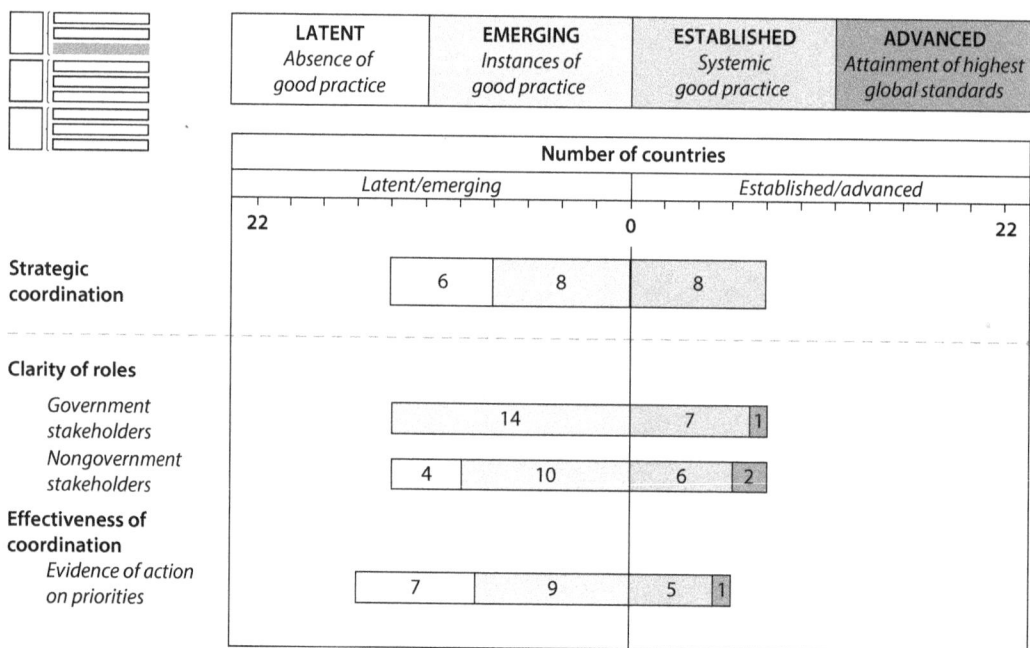

Source: World Bank construction based on data for 22 countries.

a rudimentary structure with regard to nongovernment stakeholders. Not all is bleak, however: eight countries are in the Established or Advanced groups, which is the same as the count for government stakeholders.

Coordination and implementation of strategic WfD initiatives at the leadership level is weak in most sample countries. The scores for implementation of leaders' initiatives in WfD tend to be lower than the scores for clarity of roles. An interesting question is the extent to which clarity about roles and responsibilities is essential for implementation of priority initiatives. Of the six countries rated Established or Advanced for implementation, all scored at the Established level for the clarity of roles (for either government or nongovernment stakeholders, or both). At the same time, several countries achieved low scores for implementation despite having high scores for clarity of roles and responsibilities, while countries like Malaysia and FYR Macedonia rate high for coordination and implementation without clearly defined roles for all stakeholders. A moment's reflection offers one possible explanation for these outcomes: initiatives at the leadership level often materialize as ad hoc prototypes or special projects to test new ideas or directions for possible scale-up if successful. Thus, even though well-defined formal structures may aid in the implementation of such initiatives, a more important factor is leaders' capacity to coordinate effort in their drive for results. In other words, well-defined roles and responsibilities, while advantageous, are neither necessary nor sufficient to ensure effective implementation of WfD initiatives at the leadership level.

System Oversight and Its Underpinnings

This dimension of the SABER-WfD framework examines the arrangements relating to: (1) the funding of vocational education and training (VET); (2) quality assurance of training provision and skills certification; and (3) learning pathways for skills acquisition and progression to further education and training. The distribution of countries by rating category across these three areas appears in figure 5.7.

The sample countries have more difficulty with funding policy for VET than with assuring quality or creating pathways for skills acquisition. No country in the sample scores above the Emerging level on Funding Policy, and half of the countries are in the Latent group. By contrast, on Quality Assurance, the majority of the countries score at the Emerging level, while five countries score in the top half of the rating scale, with one of them, Malaysia, achieving a score in the topmost category. The average score for Quality Assurance is in fact the highest among subdimension level scores at the same level of aggregation. With regard to Learning Pathways, countries cluster in the Emerging category, suggesting that the routes for skills acquisition tend to be limited and fragmented and thus inadequate for individuals to fulfill their aspirations for career advancement.

The next section unpacks the foregoing summary assessment by examining the underlying drivers of the three subdimension components of Funding Policy, Quality Assurance, and Learning Pathways.

Figure 5.7 System Oversight and Its Underpinnings

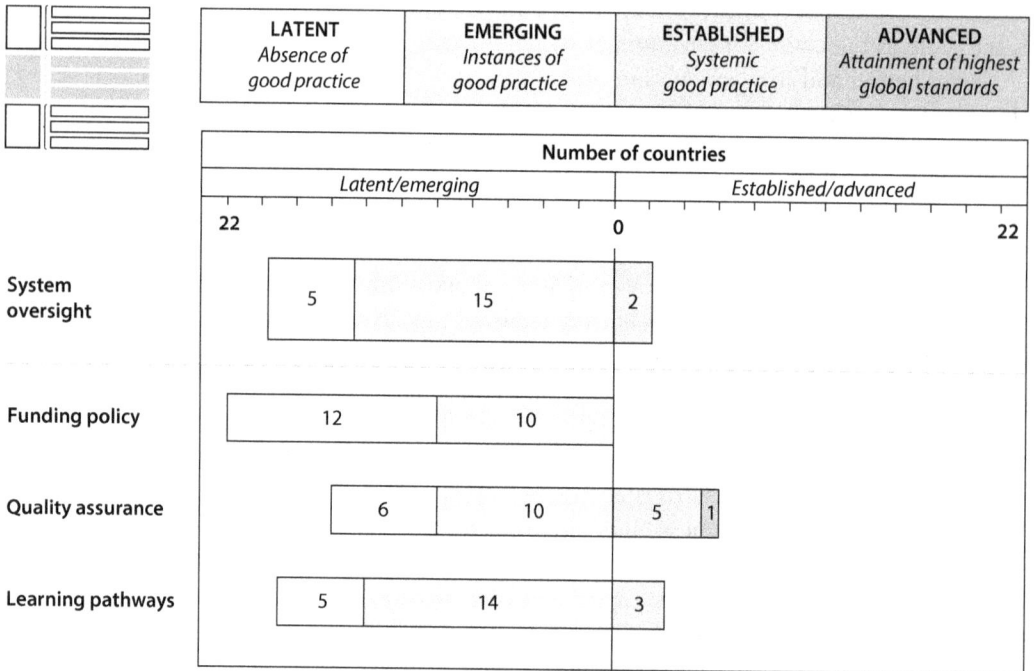

LATENT *Absence of good practice*	EMERGING *Instances of good practice*	ESTABLISHED *Systemic good practice*	ADVANCED *Attainment of highest global standards*

Number of countries

Latent/emerging | *Established/advanced*

22 | 0 | 22

	Latent	Emerging	Established	Advanced
System oversight	5	15	2	
Funding policy	12	10		
Quality assurance	6	10	5	1
Learning pathways	5	14	3	

Source: World Bank construction based on data for 22 countries.

Funding Policy

This subcomponent evaluates three aspects of funding policy: (1) the *efficiency of public funding* for skills acquisition through initial vocational education and training (IVET), continuing vocational education and training (CVET), and targeted training embedded in active labor market programs; (2) the *equity* of such funding; and (3) the mobilization of *resources from private sector partners* to support skills acquisition through any of these routes. The distribution of countries by performance category appears in figure 5.8, and its highlights follow.

Countries in the sample tend to focus more on the efficiency of public funding for WfD than on its equity. This relationship holds true for IVET, CVET, and active labor market programs, with at least half the sample rated Emerging or better for efficiency, compared to at least half rated Latent for equity. However, ratings for both efficiency and equity are low when compared to other aspects of the system. This result suggests that taking advantage of the way government money for WfD is allocated to incentivize cost-effective and equitable service delivery is either a particular challenge or a low priority across sample countries. A pervasive issue is that in almost all sample countries there are serious gaps in information on how well publicly funded programs are performing. One reason for the gaps is that reviews for impact on efficiency or equity are rarely conducted. The lack of reviews is reflected in the scores: the average score

Figure 5.8 Funding Policy and the Underlying Drivers

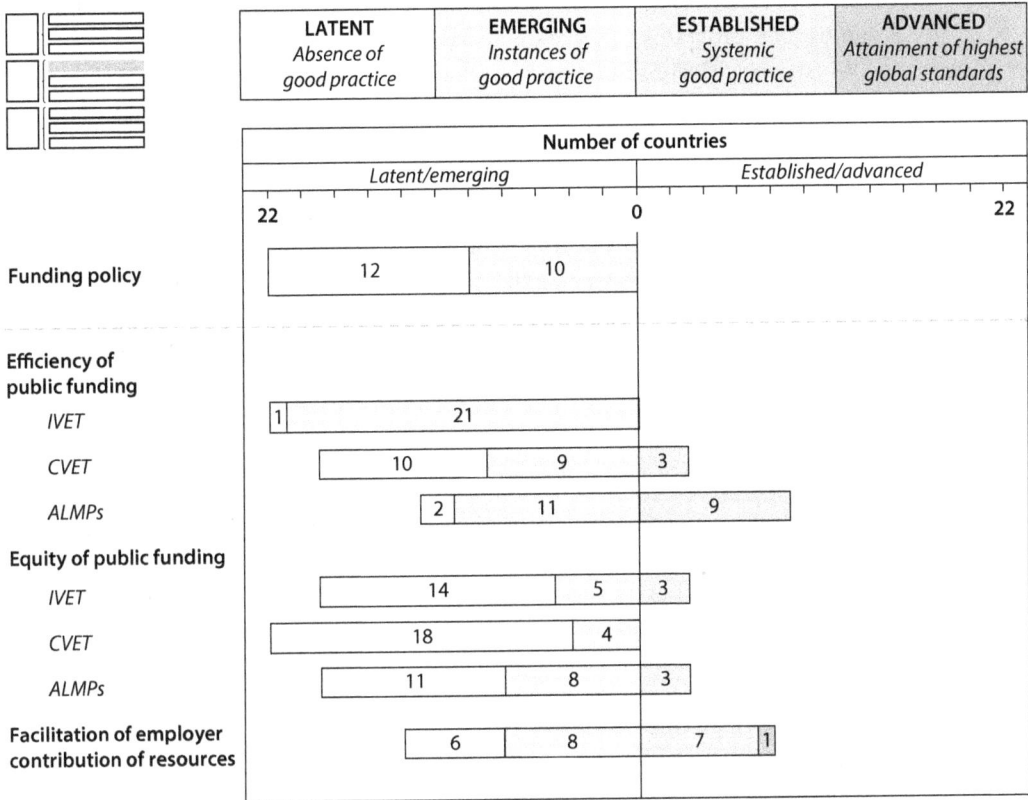

	LATENT *Absence of good practice*	EMERGING *Instances of good practice*	ESTABLISHED *Systemic good practice*	ADVANCED *Attainment of highest global standards*

Number of countries

Latent/emerging — *Established/advanced*

22 — 0 — 22

Funding policy	12 / 10
Efficiency of public funding	
IVET	1 / 21
CVET	10 / 9 / 3
ALMPs	2 / 11 / 9
Equity of public funding	
IVET	14 / 5 / 3
CVET	18 / 4
ALMPs	11 / 8 / 3
Facilitation of employer contribution of resources	6 / 8 / 7 / 1

Source: World Bank construction based on data for 22 countries.
Notes: ALMP = active labor market programs; CVET = continuing vocational education and training; IVET = initial vocational education and training.

for questions in the SABER-WfD questionnaire relating specifically to monitoring and review of policies or to the presence of special studies to determine the efficiency of system functioning is only 1.4, or Latent.

On efficiency, CVET receives the least attention among the three types of training in the sample countries. The scores for CVET cluster in the Latent category, possibly reflecting the low priority of such programs. For IVET, the score in almost every country falls in the Emerging category, a rating that recognizes the existence of formalized budgeting processes while also highlighting the haphazard consideration of the cost-effectiveness of public spending on WfD.[6] For active labor market programs, just two countries score in the Latent group, and nine are in the Established group; the better results are consistent with the smaller size and more targeted nature of active labor market programs, which are more conducive to rigorous evaluations for impact.

On equity, attention is rare for all types of training in the sample countries, even for programs intended for the poor. A rating of Latent means an absence of recent formal reviews of the impact on various socioeconomic groups of public funding for training. That so many countries fall into this group for active labor market programs is as surprising as it is worrisome, considering the stated intention of such programs to serve disadvantaged populations.

Mustering private resources is a relative bright spot in the sample countries' funding policy. These resources include in-kind and financial contributions. Six countries are rated at the Latent level, implying that these resources are largely untapped. The remaining countries in the sample have taken steps, at either the central level or the provider level, to facilitate partnerships with employers to tap these resources. Those countries scoring at the Established or Advanced level have also been able to formalize the processes by which such partnerships are set up. In all countries there is clearly room for improvement. Even in Malaysia, the one country rated Advanced, the score reflects close links mainly between public training providers and government-linked enterprises, rather than enterprises that are fully private.

Quality Assurance

The Quality Assurance component of the score for System Oversight focuses on three features of WfD systems: (1) the comprehensiveness and robustness of competency *standards*; (2) the credibility of testing and *certification of skills*; and (3) the effectiveness of protocols for setting, enforcing, and fostering *accreditation of training programs*. The results in each of these areas are summarized in figure 5.9.

Countries in the sample vary widely in their progress toward better quality assurance systems for WfD. The diversity is greater for this policy goal of the WfD system than for any of the other policy goals examined in the SABER-WfD framework. In all eight areas of Quality Assurance shown in the figure, the sample countries consistently straddle across at least three, if not all four, levels of performance. The greater number of high scores compared to other subdimension components considered in this analysis is perhaps reflective of the amount of attention that standards and qualifications frameworks have garnered in WfD policy circles in recent years. Indeed, in countries such as Bulgaria, Georgia, Grenada, and Sri Lanka, a focus on establishing coherent standards as part of putting in place national qualifications frameworks (associated, in the case of Bulgaria and Georgia, with linking with the European Qualifications Framework) has led to Established ratings, while other aspects of system governance and service delivery have received lower ratings associated with less success in formalizing and institutionalizing system processes. The diversity suggests a strong potential for learning across sample countries in setting up and strengthening arrangements for quality assurance in WfD.

Regarding standards, formal qualifications frameworks exist in most of the sample countries, but they vary widely in robustness and scope. All countries have adopted some form of competency-based standards, often with an eye to developing a national qualifications framework. However, progress has been piecemeal and halting: more than half the sample countries are still at the Latent or Emerging stage in formalizing a qualifications framework with any significant occupational coverage. The results reflect a scarcity of inclusive processes for

Figure 5.9 Quality Assurance and the Underlying Drivers

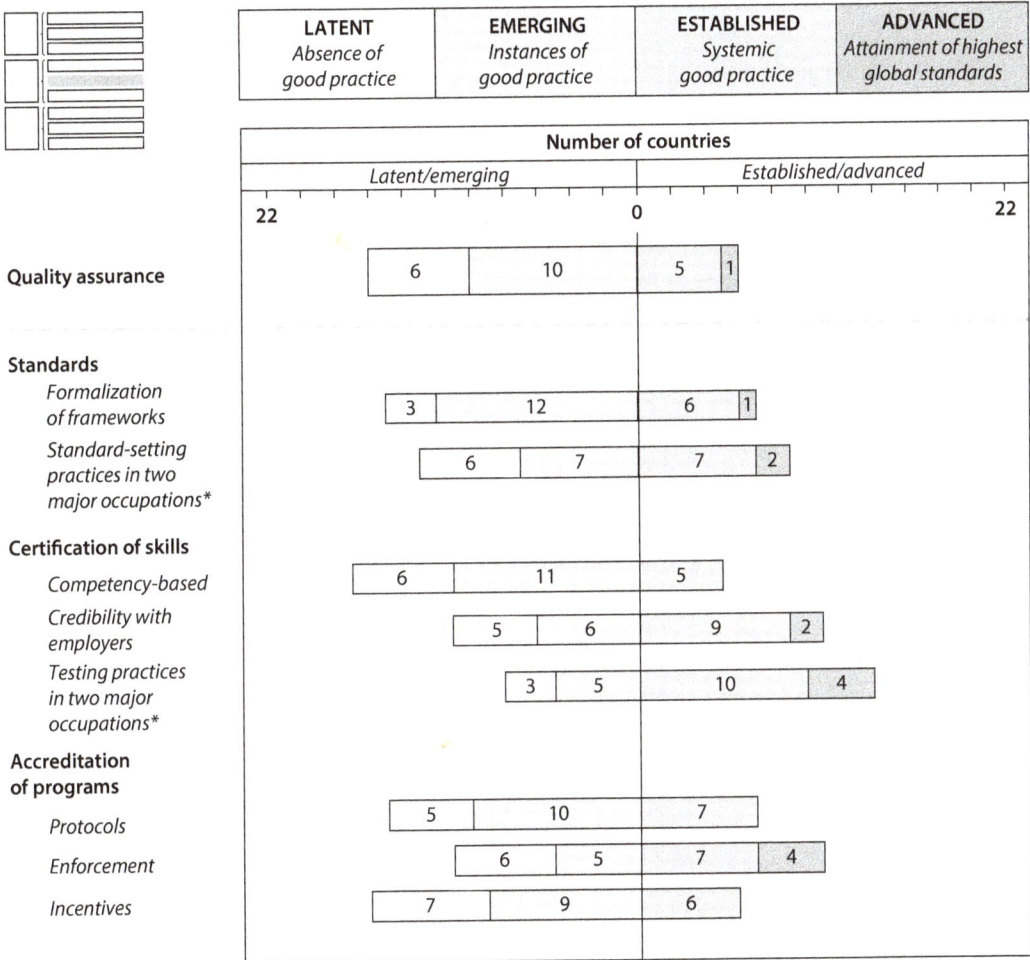

LATENT	EMERGING	ESTABLISHED	ADVANCED
Absence of good practice	*Instances of good practice*	*Systemic good practice*	*Attainment of highest global standards*

Number of countries

Latent/emerging — Established/advanced

22 — 0 — 22

Quality assurance: 6 | 10 | 5 | 1

Standards
Formalization of frameworks: 3 | 12 | 6 | 1
Standard-setting practices in two major occupations*: 6 | 7 | 7 | 2

Certification of skills
Competency-based: 6 | 11 | 5
Credibility with employers: 5 | 6 | 9 | 2
Testing practices in two major occupations*: 3 | 5 | 10 | 4

Accreditation of programs
Protocols: 5 | 10 | 7
Enforcement: 6 | 5 | 7 | 4
Incentives: 7 | 9 | 6

Source: World Bank construction based on data for 22 countries.
Note: * refers to skilled or semiskilled occupations.

specifying standards that feature, at their core, effective cooperation between industry and government. In major occupations,[7] countries either rise to the occasion, with a greater number scoring in the Established or Advanced categories, or fall further behind. In the countries scoring in the Established or Advanced categories, the result is consistent with a strategy of starting small by focusing on key industries as a way to build capacity and support for further expansion. In the lagging countries, the low scores suggest a possible lack of commitment to such a step-by-step approach.

Regarding skills certification, many countries have established the trustworthiness of common certificates and of testing for major occupations, but establishing a broader system of competency-based testing is more challenging. The score for competency-based testing gauges both how well the system is managed and its coverage (that is, how many trainees and occupations are covered by the system). No country in the sample scores at the Advanced level, and only five score at the Established level; in most of the sample countries, competency standards are defined for only a few occupations and are used only by some training providers. The scores improve for the narrower issues of gaining employers' trust in a well-defined set of commonly used certificates and of following robust procedures for skills testing in major occupations. Because creating a national qualifications system takes time, higher scores in these more specific areas are encouraging. It suggests that even as the system as a whole is still expanding and management practices are formalizing, good practices are possible in a limited number of occupations and industries.

Regarding accreditation, countries in the sample are better at enforcing existing requirements than following systematic protocols for setting and reviewing standards for getting accredited or supporting providers to meet standards. Most countries in the sample have put in place a regulatory framework for accreditation and designated an agency for setting and enforcing accreditation standards. Still, with 15 countries rated at the Emerging or Latent level for the clarity of the protocols for accreditation, this aspect of the system remains poorly developed. Few of the countries have put in place an effective package of incentives (such as linking accreditation to licensing or eligibility for public funds) and support to help training providers meet standards, especially through the robust and institutionalized mechanisms required to earn an Established rating. In contrast, a surprisingly large number of countries score at the Established or Advanced levels for enforcing existing regulations. The balance of effort appears to be struck in favor of policing the standards rather than facilitating or encouraging adherence to high standards in training provision.

Learning Pathways

Open learning pathways that allow individuals to easily enter and exit the VET system throughout their lives are critical to making VET an attractive option and enabling a country to keep abreast of rapid changes in the global economy. The subdimension scores here are based on an examination of the following: (1) arrangements for progression and transfer into and out of the *preemployment VET* system; (2) procedures that facilitate *continuing education and training*, such as recognition of prior learning and the provision of career guidance services; and (3) the availability of *programs for disadvantaged groups* that facilitate their access to skills acquisition and career building services. The distribution of countries by performance in each of these areas appears in figure 5.10, and the key highlights follow.

Regarding preemployment VET, sample countries do remarkably well in establishing open pathways for skills acquisition, but few address public skepticism about VET and the lack of program articulation. No country in the sample is rated Latent on pathways, 12 are rated Established, and three are considered Advanced. VET students in most of the sample countries can, in theory, progress to higher levels of education, including to university-level programs. But because

Figure 5.10 Learning Pathways and the Underlying Drivers

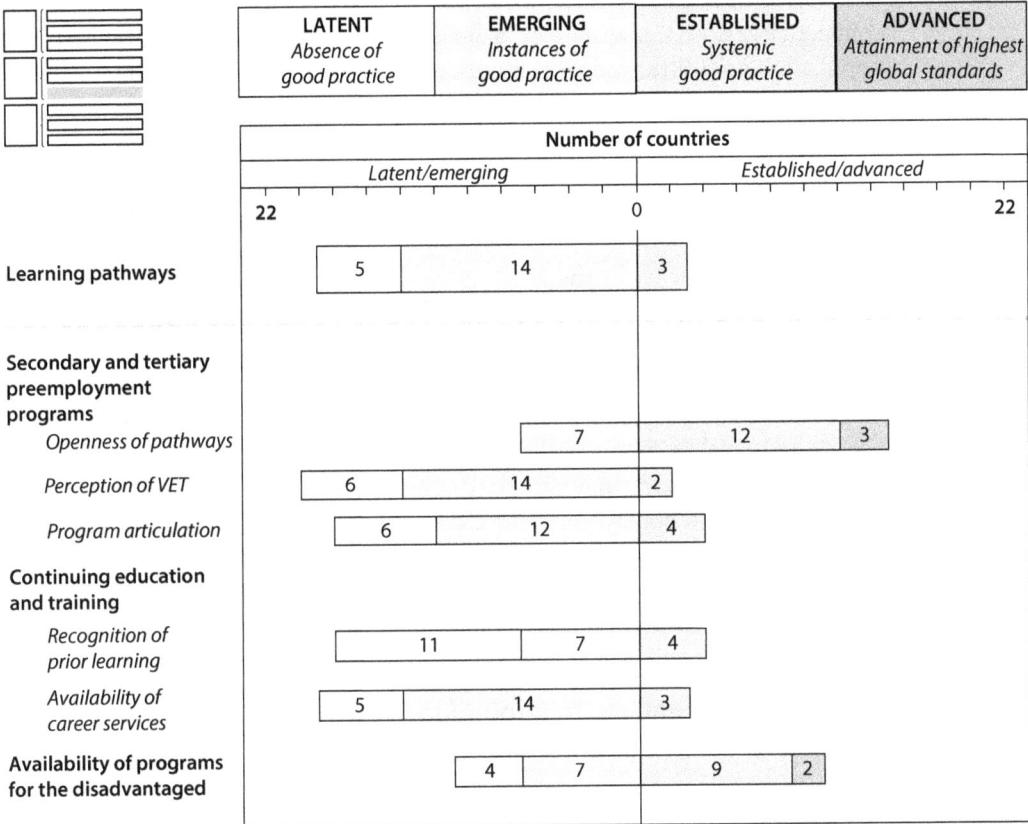

	LATENT *Absence of good practice*	EMERGING *Instances of good practice*	ESTABLISHED *Systemic good practice*	ADVANCED *Attainment of highest global standards*

Number of countries

Latent/emerging — *Established/advanced*

22 — 0 — 22

	Latent	Emerging	Established	Advanced
Learning pathways	5	14	3	
Secondary and tertiary preemployment programs				
Openness of pathways		7	12	3
Perception of VET	6	14	2	
Program articulation	6	12	4	
Continuing education and training				
Recognition of prior learning	11	7	4	
Availability of career services	5	14	3	
Availability of programs for the disadvantaged	4	7	9	2

Source: World Bank construction based on data for 22 countries.

the VET track often provides a less-rigorous preparation for university entrance examinations than is done for academic tracks, it puts VET students at a practical disadvantage for gaining entry to higher education. Few governments create formal obstacles to progression, but they also do not take active steps to facilitate progression. (Potential active steps could include improving the quality of general education delivered in VET institutions and ensuring broad recognition of vocational credentials from private and non–Ministry of Education providers within the formal education system.) In the sample of countries, only Malaysia and Turkey have taken a systematic and sustained approach to improving public perceptions of preemployment VET.

Most of the sample countries struggle with building a strong system of CVET, particularly with regard to the recognition of prior learning. Half of the sample countries score in the Latent category for recognition of prior learning, whether nonformal or informal. Performance is better in the provision of systematic support for career development to the general public, with the majority of countries clustered at the Emerging level. Even so, the score describes a situation in which services are available, but are provided through disparate stand-alone centers rather than through an integrated network benefiting from pooled resources and connectivity. CVET may not be a high priority for policy makers where the population is youthful and large numbers of young people are entering the labor market for the first time. Its importance, however, is likely to grow in situations where the population is aging or where the economy is changing rapidly. In such settings, workers will need new skills to keep up with changing job requirements and opportunities, and many are likely to delay retirement from the workforce.

Regarding programs for the disadvantaged, arrangements are diverse across the sample countries, with a relatively large number performing at the Established level. Systems that do well in this area provide systematic support for a variety of disadvantaged populations and make some provision to review the impact on outcomes for target populations. The high number of countries scoring at the Established level or better indicates that, beyond ensuring open pathways and support for continuing training and career development, governments see the provision of programs specially targeted to the disadvantaged as a core aspect of their mandate. It is noteworthy, however, that this commitment in provision is not always matched by rigorousness in confirming the equity of such targeted programs, as the scores on funding policy discussed earlier suggest.

Service Delivery and Its Underpinnings

Service Delivery, the third dimension in the SABER-WfD framework, is concerned with the functioning of the WfD system's network of public and private providers of all types of vocational education and training. The dimension-level score aggregates the ratings on three underlying drivers of performance: (1) organizational diversity and excellence in service provision; (2) relevance of programs offered by public sector providers; and (3) effectiveness in the use of data for overall system management. The distribution of countries by rating category in these three areas appears in figure 5.11.

Almost all the sample countries have difficulty operating a well-run system of training provision, one with public and private organizations accountable for and managed to achieve results in the job market. The sample countries cluster in the Emerging group across all three areas considered, with a nontrivial number in the Latent category. In each area, just one country, either Malaysia or Turkey, breaks into the Established category. The generally poor ratings are cause for concern. They point to challenges in managing public providers and assuring the quality of private providers, weaknesses that undermine the capacity of the WfD system to meet employers' and individuals' skills needs.

The next sections unpack the foregoing summary assessment to understand the underlying sources of the poor outcomes. In particular, they examine the drivers of the subdimension scores for Diversity and Excellence, Relevance of Public Programs, and System Management.

Figure 5.11 Service Delivery and Its Underpinnings

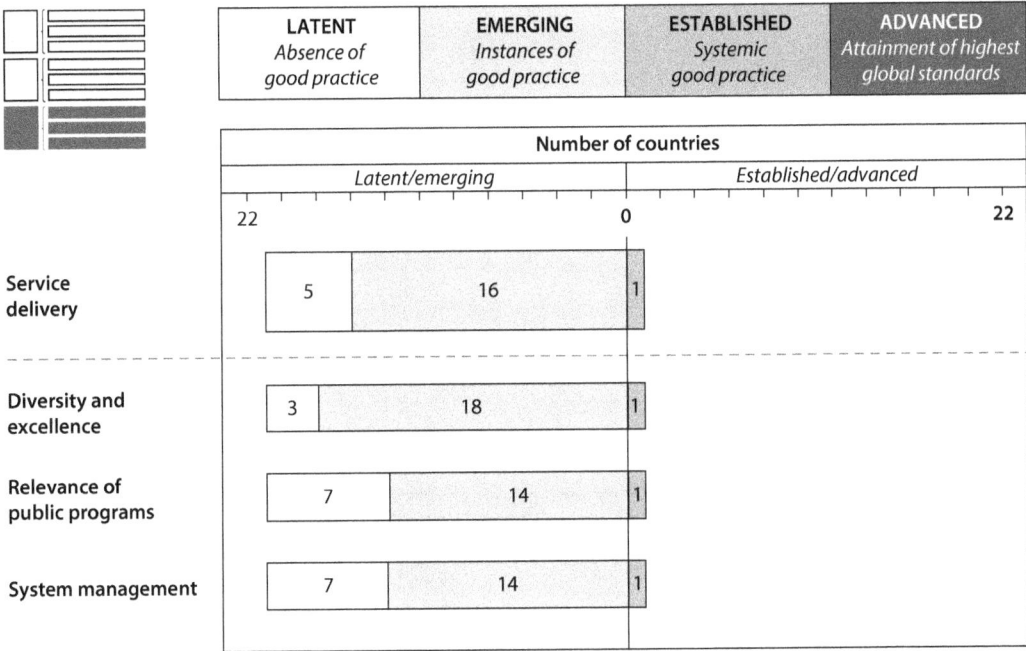

	LATENT *Absence of good practice*	EMERGING *Instances of good practice*	ESTABLISHED *Systemic good practice*	ADVANCED *Attainment of highest global standards*

	Number of countries			
	Latent/emerging		*Established/advanced*	
	22	0		22
Service delivery	5 / 16	1		
Diversity and excellence	3 / 18	1		
Relevance of public programs	7 / 14	1		
System management	7 / 14	1		

Source: World Bank construction based on data for 22 countries.

Diversity and Excellence in Training Provision

The focus here is on education and training providers, state and nonstate, and the environment in which they operate. Among nonstate providers competitive pressures drive performance, while among state providers direct competition may be less practical or feasible than measures geared toward striking an effective balance between institutional autonomy and accountability. Therefore, the SABER-WfD framework rates countries on the basis of (1) the *regulatory environment for nonstate institutions*; and (2) the procedures for supervision and management to promote the *accountability of public institutions*. The results appear in figure 5.12, and a discussion of their highlights follows.

Most sample countries have vibrant training provision by nonstate institutions governed by static policies that rely more on regulation than incentives to drive quality. No country is rated Latent for the vibrancy of its nonstate sector; in fact, the vast majority are rated Established, and four are even in the Advanced group, a rating that describes a situation characterized by the presence of a diverse set of nonstate training providers. Concerning the regulation of providers, the arrangements to identify, support, and censure providers failing to meet quality standards have reached a level of formalization and sophistication meriting an Established score in almost half the countries; in contrast, only two countries use incentives to foster quality to a level that earns an Established rating. Competitive forces play a role in fostering quality in private markets, but weaknesses in engaging providers through regulation and incentives create substantial pockets

Figure 5.12 Diversity and Excellence and the Underlying Drivers

	LATENT *Absence of good practice*	EMERGING *Instances of good practice*	ESTABLISHED *Systemic good practice*	ADVANCED *Attainment of highest global standards*

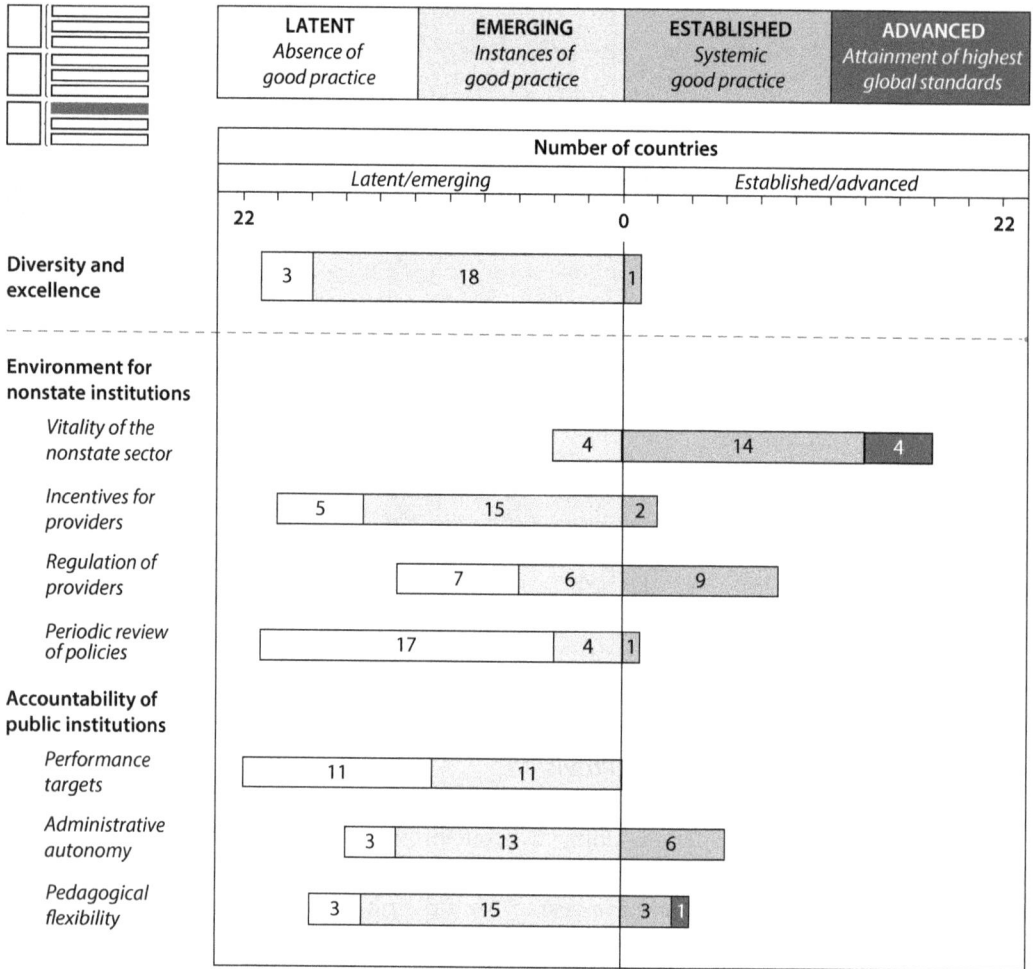

Source: World Bank construction based on data for 22 countries.

of low quality that are not being proactively addressed in many countries. This issue has not grabbed the government's attention in many countries because practically no country conducts routine reviews of policies toward nonstate institutions, and very few have undertaken any recent review.

Few sample countries manage public providers for excellence through institutional performance targets combined with flexibility over administrative and pedagogical matters. No country has a system rated Established for setting performance targets for public providers of vocational education and training. In most countries, significant parts of the public training system inputs are largely managed centrally, resulting in scores of Latent or Emerging for administrative autonomy. Similarly, few countries grant public institutions broad pedagogical flexibility to introduce, modify, and close programs. However, there are notable variations in scores for administrative and pedagogical autonomy. In countries such as Jordan, FYR Macedonia, Turkey, the Solomon Islands, St. Lucia, and Ukraine, practices score at the Established or Advanced levels in one or both of these areas. However, it is important to note that more autonomy is not necessarily preferable in the absence of performance targets and other methods to promote accountability. Although the freedom to make decisions without approval by higher authorities can enable school managers to more nimbly meet the demand for skills, in highly decentralized systems the absence of well-defined outcomes targets runs the risk of diffusing responsibility for results. In such settings, efforts to improve service provision through increased autonomy may miss the mark.

Relevance of Public Programs

Because public sector providers may be shielded from competitive market forces, governments often intervene directly to improve the relevance of programs offered by such institutions. The SABER-WfD framework considers three aspects that drive performance in this regard: (1) *links with industry*; (2) *provider connections with research institutions*; and (3) *attention to staff quality through recruitment and staff development policies*. Figure 5.13 summarizes the distribution of countries across performance groups in these areas, and an elaboration of the highlights follows.

Figure 5.13 Relevance of Public Provision and the Underlying Drivers

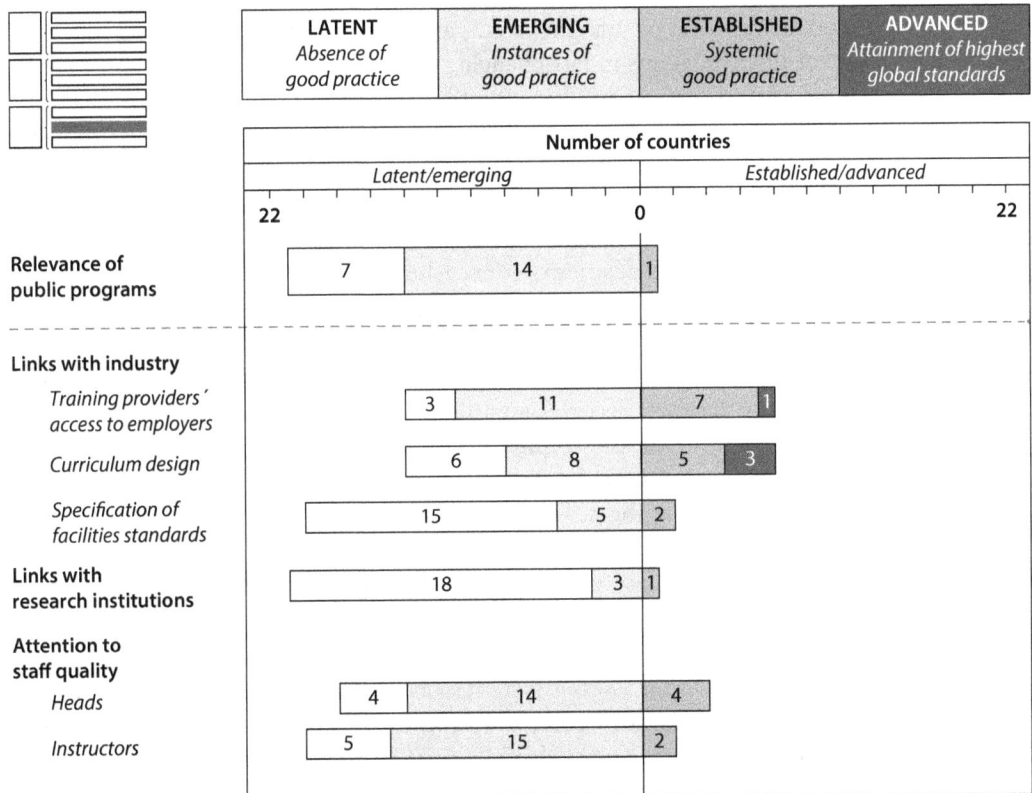

Source: World Bank construction based on data for 22 countries.

Workforce Development in Emerging Economies • http://dx.doi.org/10.1596/978-1-4648-0850-0

Provider-industry linkages are common, but often ad hoc in the sample countries, and help more with curriculum design than with specification of facilities standards. Links with industry take many forms, including partnerships for training development, internships for staff and students, and sourcing teaching staff from industry. In almost all the sample countries public training institutions have established some relationships with industry counterparts, mainly to support training delivery, but the scores for *robustness* indicate that such relationships have become widespread and formal in fewer than half the sample countries. In most cases these relationships are limited to advising on skills needs or providing internship or apprenticeship placements. In approximately two-thirds of the sample countries, collaboration extends to curriculum development, but rarely do employers provide input in setting facility standards.

Provider-research links are rare among the sample countries and are limited to those countries that are more economically developed. Such links benefit training providers by enlarging their capacity to renew course curricula to keep abreast of technology developments and market trends. Among the sample countries, only Malaysia has an Established rating for this aspect of the WfD system. There, a university that has traditionally trained VET instructors has taken the lead role in developing and implementing instructor training programs aligned to national competency-based occupational standards. In the absence of partnerships with industry and research institutions, providers are left to operate with limited information on training needs, a problem that can undermine the relevance of their programs in fast-changing environments.

Staff quality receives modest attention among the sample countries, despite its potential role in enlarging public institutions' capacity to deliver industry relevant programs. For both the heads of such institutions and instructors, most countries are clustered in the Emerging groups. This rating reflects staffing policies that require personnel to have a relevant background, either through teaching or through industry experience, but offer few opportunities for professional development, especially opportunities that would increase exposure to the state-of-the-art in their relevant industries. It is alarming that in a small but not negligible set of countries, ensuring that instructors have relevant experience in teaching or industry receives no attention at the policy level. Anecdotal evidence from several sample countries with low scores in this area suggests that prestige and compensation are constraints to recruiting qualified staff. Therefore, a focus on improving the selectiveness of instructor recruitment may not yield the desired results in the absence of efforts to overcome the broader issues of adequate funding for and public skepticism of VET.

System Management

The SABER-WfD tool assesses system management based on the WfD system's culture of data collection, utilization, and dissemination to drive performance at the level of training providers. It examines effort in three specific areas: (1) *administrative data reporting* to track training providers' achievement of tangible outcomes, variously measured; (2) *periodic in-depth analyses* and selective testing of promising ideas for improvement and cross-fertilization across institutions; and (3) evidence of *data-driven system improvement* involving a dynamic of systematic learning and progress. The scores for the sample countries on these facets of their WfD systems appear in figure 5.14, which is followed by a discussion of their highlights.

Data-driven system management is nascent in the sample countries. Few countries rely on in-depth analyses and systematic feedback for dynamic learning and improvement. Fewer than half of the countries regularly collect and maintain administrative data from both public and private providers in a centralized database; for the rest, data reporting by providers is fragmented or incomplete. When administrative data are collected, few countries require providers to report on indicators such as job placement rates, earnings of graduates, or client feedback, information that is crucial for individuals selecting VET programs and for provider institutions seeking to identify program areas for improvement.

Furthermore, few countries supplement the administrative data they collect with in-depth analyses, special surveys, or studies. Among the 22 sample countries, only Malaysia has routine, institutionalized processes for conducting in-depth assessments of special topics. Overall, there is little evidence that countries make routine use of data for systemic and proactive management of training provider performance (such as identifying leading institutions as models for learning or lagging institutions for targeted support).

Figure 5.14 System Management and the Underlying Drivers

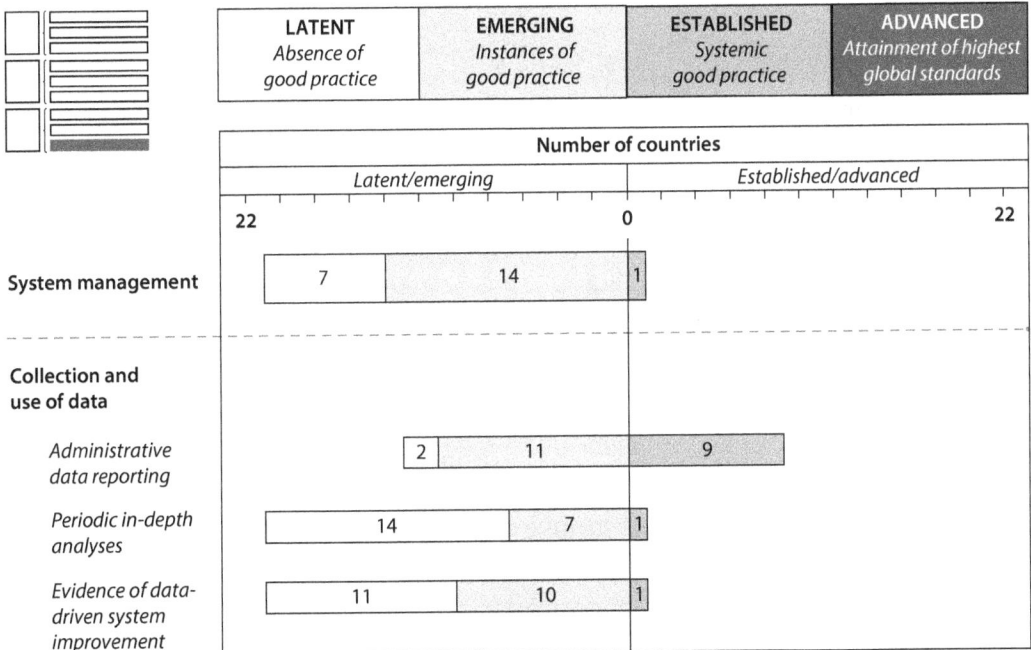

Source: World Bank construction based on data for 22 countries.

Workforce Development in Emerging Economies • http://dx.doi.org/10.1596/978-1-4648-0850-0

Summary of Key Highlights for the 22 Countries

For each country, the foregoing SABER-WfD results reveal the state of policies, institutions, and praxis. They highlight successes to build on and lagging areas that may need reform. The results are a starting point for in-country policy dialogue about the way forward. To varying degrees, such dialogue has already taken place in all 22 countries in the sample. The SABER-WfD results also shed light on common challenges across countries as well as areas that pose relatively few difficulties. To the extent that these findings depict the status of WfD systems more generally among emerging economies, they can help sharpen international dialogue on and support for strengthening WfD systems in such settings.

The 22 countries have SABER-WfD scores that generally cluster at the Emerging level, implying that these countries have yet to institutionalize most of the good practices that characterize high-performing WfD systems. The scores paint the following picture:

- With regard to Strategic Framework, the task of forming and sustaining strategic partnerships with employers appears to be more challenging than that of articulating a direction for WfD or ensuring coordination of effort on specific priorities.
- With regard to System Oversight, ensuring equitable and efficient funding for VET poses more difficulty than assuring quality or creating pathways for skills acquisition.
- With regard to Service Delivery, putting in place regulation, incentives, and monitoring to ensure that public and private organizations are accountable for and managed to achieve results in the job market is a common challenge.

Although all areas of the WfD systems in the 22 countries need to improve, some areas may benefit from especially close attention. Unpacking the dimension-level scores into their underlying drivers shed additional light on the prevalence of low scores and the experience of countries with stronger systems. The key highlights in this regard appear in figure 5.15, based on the fuller summary in table A.1. Under the Strategic Framework dimension, the pattern in the scores emphasizes the need to foster genuine partnerships with employers on strategic priorities for WfD and to focus on effective implementation of such priorities. Under the System Oversight dimension, the scores underline the need to examine and improve equity in public spending on skills development, to destigmatize social perceptions about VET, and to strengthen program articulation to enhance options in learning pathways for skills acquisition. Finally, under the Service Delivery dimension, the results call for consideration of the role of incentives, as a complement to regulation, to encourage private providers to meet quality standards for service provision; the setting of performance targets in public training institutions to improve the efficiency and effectiveness of such institutions; and expanded use of data-driven management across the WfD system.

Figure 5.15 Highlights of SABER-WfD Findings for 22 Countries

Strategic framework	Advocacy for WfD is substantive but lacks high-level advocates' sustained, vocal support.
	Partnership with employers falters because of inadequate governance structures.
	Critical WfD initiatives yield few results for lack of attention to effective implementation.

System oversight	Equity of funding for skills development receives insufficient attention.
	Formal standards for skills certification and accreditation are reasonably developed.
	Learning pathways are open, but VET stigma and program articulation remain issues.

Service delivery	Private provision is vibrant and typically operates under passive government regulation.
	Performance targets are not emphasized in public institutions.
	Data are rarely used systematically to track, evaluate, and improve system performance.

Source: World Bank distillation of the results discussed in this chapter and summarized more fully in table A.1.
Note: SABER = Systems Approach for Better Education Results; "VET stigma" refers to negative social perceptions about vocational education and training as compared with academic programs; WfD = workforce development.

Notes

1. The data for the 22 countries were collected using the same version of the question-naire, thus allowing comparisons at all levels of data aggregation. Excluded from the full sample of 27 countries and the West Bank and Gaza (listed in footnote 2 in chapter 1) were the following six countries for which data were collected using an earlier version of the questionnaire: Chile, Korea, Ireland, Singapore, Uganda, and Vietnam.

2. Among the nine counties, only Iraq, facing considerable barriers related to ongoing conflict, scores at the Latent level for all three dimensions.

3. The score for the first of these two factors is based on the level of engagement in advocacy for WfD as an important national policy issue by both government and nongovernment leaders and the formality of mechanisms for collaboration among these leaders for determining strategic priorities. The score for the second factor—relating to the substantive content of the advocacy—is based on the breadth of priorities on which specific actions have been identified and the tangibility of decisions on action to support strategic priorities. This careful process of aggregat-ing the underlying data collected by the SABER-WfD questionnaire is applied to the data for all the other areas to be discussed; to manage the length of this report, they are not elaborated. For further details, interested readers are referred to SABER-WfD framework paper (World Bank 2013) and the SABER-WfD data collection instrument.

4. The score for the first driver is based on information about the availability, scope, and reliability of surveys and studies on the direction of economic development and its implications for skills. For the second driver, the score gauges the involvement of employers in setting WfD strategy and measures taken by the government to activate and engage these important system stakeholders.

5. The HRDF is funded through a mandatory levy of 1 percent of the monthly wage bill for all enterprises above a threshold number of employees that varies by economic sector.

6. Countries use various indicators to assess the cost-effectiveness of public spending, among them the following: completion rates, job placement rates of graduates, and capacity for provider innovation in service delivery.

7. The major occupations were identified by the researcher through extensive consultations with system stakeholders in each country.

Reference

World Bank. 2013. "What Matters for Workforce Development: A Framework and Tool for Analysis." SABER Working Paper 6, World Bank, Washington, DC.

CHAPTER 6

SABER-WfD and the Agenda for Systems Development

The Systems Approach for Better Education Results-Workforce Development (SABER-WfD) was created as part of a suite of tools to facilitate implementation of the World Bank's 10-year Education Sector Strategy, which was launched in 2012. Like other SABER tools, it is based on the premise that systems development is at the heart of what is required to support emerging economies in enhancing education and training outcomes. It focuses on institutions and praxis to draw attention to the mechanisms through which policies are implemented. Gaining traction on this important agenda faces headwinds, however, for two reasons: (1) systems development is an amorphous and multifaceted concept that is open to multiple interpretations, and (2) building systems is inevitably time-consuming. The concept's vagueness can distract and impede policy dialogue, particularly dialogue about WfD systems, where the interlocutors involved are both numerous and diverse in their roles, expectations, and experiences. The fact that it takes time to build systems—often decades rather than years—adds to the difficulty, in part because differences in understanding and perception arise more easily on how systems and their constituent components grow, evolve, and mature over time.

The SABER-WfD tool offers one approach for lowering these barriers to a productive dialogue. Its conceptual framework, common terminology, and standardized data collection protocols have enabled the comparative analysis presented in this book, based on their application in 27 countries and the West Bank and Gaza, entities where diverse stakeholders were engaged in validating and reflecting on the polity-specific findings. The process and results obtained have affirmed the tool's potential for deepening our understanding of WfD systems and the institutional underpinnings that influence their performance. This section reflects on how emerging economies and their development partners—including multilateral and bilateral organizations, both public and private, as well as domestic entities—might use the tool to engage in knowledge exchange and policy action to strengthen WfD systems and their impact on building job-relevant skills.

Broadening the Dialogue

The Sustainable Development Goals (SDGs) for 2030 reaffirm the role of education while expanding its scope to include the more ambitious aim of enhancing learning and job-relevant skills. Between 2000 and 2015, the Millennium Development Goals (MDGs) focused policy makers' attention on just eight targets, among them universalizing primary education by 2015.[1] Much has been achieved under the impetus of the MDGs, as reflected in rising gross enrollment ratios, from an average of about 80 percent among low-income countries in 2000 to levels already exceeding 100 percent by 2010. The SDGs for 2030 are more expansive: 17 items in total, among them the objective to "ensure inclusive and equitable quality education and promote lifelong learning opportunities for all." This goal makes explicit mention of "affordable and quality technical, vocational, and tertiary education," and "relevant skills, including technical and vocational skills, for employment, decent jobs and entrepreneurship."[2]

The SDGs' implicit skills-and-jobs agenda will require the education sector to work more closely and collaboratively with entities outside the sector, notably the economic ministries and the business community. Under the MDGs, the education goal aimed at a population-based target (namely, universal coverage of primary education), which is relatively static. Under the SDGs, the target is linked to the labor market and its demand for skills, thus requiring the education and training system to be attuned to signals from beyond the education sector if it is to be effective. Because labor market conditions are seldom static, establishing targets this way is required on an almost permanent basis.

Broadening the canvas for policy dialogue beyond the education sector brings into focus skills initiatives taking place elsewhere that may be highly relevant but otherwise ignored. Such activity can be significant: a 2011 World Bank review, for example, documents the existence of project-related training in a great diversity of operations, including agriculture, environment, and private sector development. Such training absorbed an estimated one-quarter to one-third of project funds in the projects examined (Valerio and Vasconcellos 2011). Although much of the training is short-term and ad hoc, some components offer promising avenues for scaling up best practices to strengthen the system for WfD. The $80 million Mexico Information Technology Industry Development Project, approved in 2008 with $38.3 million in World Bank financing devoted to skills development to enhance industry competitiveness, is an example (Sudan 2013). As of 2013, under a governance arrangement involving the government, information technology industry associations, and a consortium of education institutions, the project had delivered the following results: 42,000 individuals trained; 34,000 trainees certified in 16 specializations related to the information technology industry; a menu of 287 different technology certifications, and 40 national certifications, all of which are updated according to industry standards; as well as a partnership with iCarnegie, a training strategy provider associated with Carnegie Mellon University, for a "Train the Trainers" program for 800 Mexican university professors (Sudan 2013).[3]

A more expansive approach to the skills-and-job agenda is already evident in recent policy dialogue at both the international and the local levels. It resonates, for example, in the way knowledge and skills are discussed in the 2014 African Transformation Report—entitled "Growing with Depth"—issued by the ACET (African Center for Economic Transformation), a leading Africa-based think tank. Although that report focuses mainly on Africa's economic strategy and targets the continent's economic policy makers as its primary audience, its discussion on building the technical knowledge and skills of Africa's workforce makes it clear that such investments—wherever they occur in the education and training system or not—must be aligned with the broader agenda for economic transformation. Similarly, the Program on Skills in Applied Sciences, Engineering and Technology, launched in 2013 by African governments with the support of the World Bank and the African Development Bank, recognizes the need for cross-sector cooperation and alignment to ensure that investments in skills are geared to support countries' priority economic sectors.

Integrating WfD into Strategies for Economic Transformation

Economic transformation is about countries making the transition from low-productivity ("traditional") activities to high-productivity ("modern") ones. Hidalgo *et al.* (2007) emphasize diversifying and increasing the sophistication of exports, which involves branching out into product spaces at adjacent yet higher levels of technological complexity. Lin and Monga (2012) encourage learning from countries with similar endowments, but higher income levels, and prioritizing support to sectors or industries associated with exports from such countries with strong track records (see also Hausmann and Klinger 2006, 2007). Being able to produce and export more sophisticated products and services entails mastery over a range of activities (Rodrik 2008; Weiss 2005). That such mastery requires investment in skills is widely acknowledged (e.g., ACET 2014; ADB 2009 and 2014; ILO 2010; World Bank 2012a, b). Yet, because skills are only one aspect of the overall agenda for economic transformation, they tend to receive less attention than needed to provide effective guidance to the relevant line ministries, including the ministries of education and training or labor.

Mission-oriented programs of technical training aimed at stretching existing technological capabilities have featured in the economic strategies of countries whose industrial policy has been successful. Box 6.1 highlights key ideas from the extensive literature on industrial policy and its link to workforce development.[4] Because experience with vocational education and training (VET) in emerging economies is decidedly uneven (e.g., Benson, Gospel, and Zhu 2013; Martinez-Fernandez and Choi 2013), caution is appropriate when committing government support for such programs as part of industrial policy. Close collaboration between training providers and firms in the prioritized industries or sectors is critical for success. It provides specific market intelligence, not just information, about the industry- or sector-specific skills required, and it creates a crucial link to prospective employers for graduates of training programs.

Box 6.1 Industrial Policy and Workforce Skills

Industrial policy refers to an approach to state stewardship of the economy in which the government offers more support to some economic activities or industries than others in pursuit of national goals. Skeptics challenge the rationale for giving the government such a prominent role in directing economic activity and draw on the checkered history of the approach to buttress their opposition. They also argue that bureaucrats are poor at "picking winners," that state action is prone to political capture, and that the public sector is ponderous and lacks the omniscience and capability to manage inherently dynamic and complicated processes (e.g., Noland and Pack 2002; Pack 2011; Pack and Saggi 2006).

Advocates of industrial policy point to East Asian countries' experience in the last 50 years as well as parallels from the earlier history of developed countries; their activist policies have triggered and sustained a growth process that has shifted production and exports in the direction of goods and services of higher value and technological sophistication (e.g., Block and Keller 2011; Lall 2000; Mazzucato 2011; Reinert 2010; Rodrik 1999). Inspired in part by these examples, many emerging economies have been pursuing some form of industrial policy, whether implicit or otherwise (see examples in Altenburg 2011 and Devlin and Moguillansky 2013). In the wake of the global financial crisis of 2007–08, the approach has regained respectability in developed countries, notably in Europe, as anxieties grow about globalization, deindustrialization, unemployment, and loss of competitiveness (e.g., Bailey, Lenihan, and Arauzo-Carod 2011; Dhéret and Morosi 2014; Stiglitz, Lin, and Mongga 2013). And in countries as diverse as China, Germany, Japan, and the United States, industrial policy is being used to foster "green" growth (Rodrik 2014).

The current debate about industrial policy has moved beyond questions of whether countries should pursue industrial policy. More attention is now being paid to the practical issues of "what" and "how" and raising questions such as: What sectors or industries might warrant support? What mix of instruments should be deployed? How should one design decision-making processes to enhance the prospects for success? How can one strike the right balance between doing too little and intervening too much? (Aiginger 2014; Altenburg 2011; Devlin and Moguillansky 2013; Nübler 2011).

The link between industrial policy and workforce development follows logically from the identification of a country's priority economic sectors. Global value chain analysis of the chosen sectors is one technique for assessing the skills required by a country to participate in or move to the more lucrative activities in the relevant global production chains (Fernandez-Stark, Bamber, and Gereffi 2011a, b; Psilos and Gereffi 2011). University-level training and research activities will often be critical and indeed tend to receive emphasis in the literature (Mazzoleni and Nelson 2009; Yusuf, Saint, and Nabeshima 2009). Experience in countries with successful industrial policy in the past few decades, such as the Republic of Korea, Singapore, and Taiwan, China, is a reminder of the complementary role of non-university technical and vocational training with a practical orientation. This realization explains why the newly launched Partnership for Skills in Applied Sciences, Engineering and Technology in Africa promotes a "continuum of scientific and technical skills... from upper secondary/technical/vocational training through to the post graduate level and scientific research" (PASET 2015).

Such collaboration does not always require explicit government intervention. In India, for example, information technology giants with a global reach, such as Infosys and Wipro, operate their own large-scale training facilities to supply the skills required by their businesses (e.g., Padmini, Bharadway, and Nair 2009; Wadhwa, de Vitton, and Gereffi 2008). Often, however, triggering and sustaining the collaboration requires government facilitation and involvement. One reason is that existing providers may lack the knowledge or experience to offer credible programs, especially in areas of skills development that are new or technologically challenging. Moreover, the training may be capital-intensive, making it unaffordable for individuals or unfeasible (or unattractive) for firms to organize their own training programs, particularly if these firms are at risk of losing their trained workers to other firms.

Public-private collaboration on mission-oriented training, although not well-documented in the literature on industrial policy, is in fact common practice in both developed and developing countries. Examples include the Costa Rican government's collaboration with Intel (MIGA 2006; Spar 1998); the collaboration between Malaysia's Penang Skills Development Centre and a consortium of foreign investors in the electronics industry (Ansu and Tan 2012); and the City Colleges of Chicago's partnership with industry leaders through the College to Careers initiative in an effort to boost the quality and volume of skills for emerging fields in the city's economy.[5] These experiences highlight several key goals of public-private collaboration in training with a focus on technological upgrading or economic catch-up: creating a pipeline of appropriately trained workers, defining common training standards that enjoy the confidence of lead firms and their subcontractors in the target industries or sectors, tapping into industry expertise to define the curriculum content and keep it current, sourcing for experts with industry experience to teach at least some of the classes, sharing the cost of the training programs, and disseminating good practices and know-how.

Mission-oriented vocational education and training is one way to accumulate knowledge and capabilities through a process of learning by doing. Transforming the structure of production and exports toward greater complexity entails a "major process of accumulation of knowledge and capabilities, both at the level of individuals and organizations" (Cimoli, Dosi, and Stiglitz 2009, 3). Mission-oriented vocational education and training offers opportunities for this process at both levels. The graduates of such training programs acquire skills and competencies that increase their chances of employment at firms in the target industries or sectors. But just as important, the activity enables the training organizations to acquire institutional capabilities for solving the myriad practical problems that inevitably arise in the attempt to foster job-relevant skills in technologically demanding fields: creating industry-relevant training curricula and sustaining their relevance in dynamic settings; mastering pedagogical approaches required to produce graduates with the right mix of cognitive, technical, and soft skills; linking graduates to job opportunities; exercising management of institutional functions such as staff development and cost and quality control, and so on. The practical nature of these capabilities implies that mastery is invariably gained through learning by doing, disciplined use of feedback from monitoring and evaluation for continuous improvement, and accountability for results (ILO 2008; Inter-Agency Working Group on TVET Indicators 2012).

For the education and training system as a whole, the real benefit of mission-oriented training programs and institutions lies in their role as exemplars or sources of ideas and standards for providers in the rest of the system. Although such programs and institutions may start off as islands of excellence in the provision of modern technical and vocational training, they achieve their full impact when the capabilities they have acquired are disseminated and replicated across the whole system. Industry- or sector-specific technical and vocational skills are part of what it takes to deepen the technological capabilities of firms and thereby increase their ability to produce and export more sophisticated and higher-value-added goods and services. Because costs, knowledge gaps, scale limitations, or other factors may prevent existing training providers from supplying such skills, the government can help by playing a facilitating role. It can do so by providing seed funding for mission-oriented training, for example in the form of specialized training programs, institutes of technology, centers of excellence, or similar types of institutions, and by convening lead firms in the target industry or sector and mobilizing their partnership in these training activities (Rodrik 2008; Weiss 2005). Given their focus on facilitating economic catch-up, such investments may be small in scale relative to the rest of the training system. Yet, if pursued in the spirit of learning by doing, they offer the means to codify the practical know-how for enhancing system-wide capabilities in the provision of training in technologically demanding areas of skills development.

Nurturing WfD Systems toward Maturity

Because it takes years, if not decades, to build well-functioning and mature WfD systems, to do so requires intentional, patient support by emerging economies' development partners. Unlike the education MDG, which focuses on a population-based target, delivering on the education-and-skills-related SDG will require strong institutions, especially those required to enable and sustain dynamic alignment between skills demand and supply. The difficulty cannot be underestimated: absence of clear successes, particularly in preparing young people for jobs through VET, prompts the observation that "[s]kills development arguably is the most difficult subsector to organize and manage in the education sector. It cuts across organizational boundaries, caters to diverse clients, involves multiple delivery systems, and keeps changing in market characteristics" (ADB 2008, 28).

Institutional reform in the VET subsector is challenging in part because it requires governance arrangements for decision making at multiple levels that involve cross-sector collaboration. Although it is a part of the education system, the VET subsector must be oriented with laser-sharp clarity around two requirements that are critical for success: (1) being attuned and responsive to the labor market and employers' demand for skills; and (2) being able to deliver effective services at a reasonable cost. Satisfying these requirements is not easy. It calls for a fundamental shift in mindsets and organization, essentially by taking advantage of approaches that more typically belong to the world of business than to education. As Collins (2005) argues, business thinking alone is insufficient; two other essential ingredients are (1) putting in place the right leaders with autonomy to act and accountability for results and (2) following disciplined operational practices.

Ireland's experience with Regional Technical Colleges exemplifies the role of new leadership in driving institutional reform. These colleges were first established in 1969 to train large numbers of school leavers as part of the country's strategy to attract foreign direct investment in several priority economic sectors. Because they were seen as forward-looking centers of innovation, their first presidents were selected accordingly: youthful, dynamic, and creative people who "were not immersed in the prevailing culture and ethos of existing higher education institutions" (O'Hare 2008, 333). Granted considerable freedoms and "untrammeled by the traditions of the older colleges and universities," these leaders in turn created middle-level technician-training programs in science, engineering, business, and art and design, with the applied emphases valued by employers. They worked closely with business and government, participating actively in efforts both to promote Ireland to foreign investors and to understand their skills requirements. The new Regional Technical College programs attracted large numbers of school leavers and were considered hugely successful in the country's industrial development (O'Hare 2008).[6]

City Colleges of Chicago (CCC) exemplifies use of business tools to improve the system's operational effectiveness and efficiency.[7] In 2010 the CCC system embarked on a sweeping reform effort called Reinvention, bringing on a new leader who came from a successful career in industry. Its focus on success is guided by performance goals for students, including labor market outcomes, and by goals for the institution's organizational health. The latter included an intensified focus on operational discipline and excellence in financial management, which led to improvements in procurement processes. The savings amounted to $41 million in operations costs between 2010 and 2012. The reform also led to the use of efficient arrangements when enlisting the expertise of industry partners to review curriculum and ensure that it aligned with available jobs in growing fields. Each industry cluster interacts with only one of CCC's seven constituent colleges on these matters, which enables its members to concentrate and share industry expertise and know-how through a single point of contact with the system, thus conserving a highly limited resource. In turn, the focal college serves as the repository of industry-benchmarked curricula and teaching resources for that particular industry to benefit students and staff in the entire system.

These examples illustrate the innovations in organization and praxis that will often be needed to strengthen WfD systems at their weakest points, typically the VET subsector. These innovations share the ingredients of visionary leadership, sustained focus, and an intentional reorientation of mindsets and incentives through reforms that see VET as a vital and distinct part of a well-functioning

WfD system. That such efforts are often long and arduous argues for sustained support by the development community. It also argues for careful calibration to ensure that such support builds ownership and capacity, using realistic milestones to track progress toward a mature, high-performing system. In such a system, VET institutions, broadly defined, would be striving to deliver high-quality programs benchmarked to industry standards while ensuring that resources are used efficiently to deliver value at reasonable cost to trainees, employers, and taxpayers. Patient support and adequate capital for institutional innovation and learning are two important avenues through which the international development community can nurture country-led initiatives to move WfD systems in the desired direction.

Building Capacity for Sustained Reform

For decades the development community has supported efforts to improve vocational education and training in emerging countries, but the results have been disappointing. The results have neither lived up to expectations (e.g., Gill, Fluitman, and Dar 2000; World Bank 1991) nor offered unequivocal evidence on what works (World Bank 2012b). Perhaps reflecting the mixed record, World Bank operations providing dedicated support to VET have been relatively modest for many years. Between 1990 and 2009 new commitments for such operations totaled $2.7 billion, just 5.5 percent of the total entering the education sector portfolio during the period.[8] In more recent years, in response to the growing interest of the Bank's partner countries, there has been a resurgence of operations supporting VET or skills development, all of it designed with an explicit focus on ensuring close links between such investments and labor market signals and industry needs.[9]

High costs and low responsiveness to employers' demand for skills remain perennial challenges, despite voluminous research and debate. The volume of analytical effort in recent years has prompted some observers to describe it as a "glut" of global reports in 2012 (NORRAG 2013). It is beyond the scope of this book to reflect on and summarize this rich and extensive debate and its implications for setting priorities for donor support for VET in emerging economies. What the SABER-WfD framework highlights is the importance of supporting countries to strengthen WfD institutions and enhance praxis at multiple levels in the system. Although capacity building is often a staple of VET projects, it tends to focus on boosting implementation of project activities and management of project-supported institutions and agencies. Too little attention has been paid to enhancing countries' capacity for strategic decision making, thus perpetuating the risk of what some have described as "policy borrowing"—adopting ideas from more developed countries without fully understanding the institutional factors required for success in building job-relevant skills (Mehrota 2009; Philips 1989; Raffe 2011).

Building countries' own capacity for decision making and policy implementation among VET leaders and practitioners across countries is essential to achieving successful reforms. Peer-to-peer learning is an especially credible source of insights into issues that might be elusive to grasp or communicate in the abstract.[10] The SABER-WfD results suggest that leadership for workforce development and governance arrangements are areas of particular weakness in most WfD systems in emerging economies. What does "sustained, vocal support by high-level advocates" or "genuine partnership with employers" look like?[11] What might these conditions accomplish? What influence might they have on the all-important challenge of ensuring that VET programs are responsive to market signals and the demand for skills? For some aspects of the work of practitioners, answers in the form of tangible examples speak more loudly than technical explanations. For this reason the World Bank facilitates occasional study visits as a strategic resource within the scope of its work. The next paragraphs summarize lessons from three study visits to Singapore between 2006 and 2009 to learn about its approach in aligning education and training with the country's economic strategy.[12]

Between 2006 and 2009 the World Bank facilitated a program of three study visits to Singapore for high-level African policy makers from the education sector and other ministries. Below are insights from the country's experience since independence in 1965 in aligning education and training with the country's economic strategy.

Singapore's leaders see a two-way mutually reinforcing link between education and training on the one hand and the economy on the other. Their "whole-of-government" approach to decision making—for both strategic and operational matters—encourages cooperation across administrative silos and minimizes misalignment of purpose. It brings into the same frame of reference policy makers' attention with regard to budget allocations and accountability for creating a skilled workforce to grow the economy.

Clarity is essential when a poor country has to tackle a big problem. In the 1960s, when mass unemployment loomed in Singapore, building sophisticated skills was hardly a priority. Instead, the first order of business was to attract *any* foreign company that could provide employment, even as the country began laying a foundation in basic education. Only later, when unemployment receded and Singapore's reputation as a reliable place for foreigners to do business was established, did attention shift to attracting technologically advanced industries and to enlarging the system's capacity to supply the higher order skills on a strong foundation of literacy and numeracy. A prominent Singapore university leader observed that perhaps the single most important lesson from the Singapore experience was to "allow the education system to evolve with the GDP."

Vocational education and training is a challenge in practically every country. Managed well, it can supply a skilled workforce to serve industry needs; in reality, however, VET often languishes as the last resort for academic laggards with no place else to go in the system. In the early 1980s VET in Singapore was just such a quagmire, shunned by students and held in low esteem by the public. In 1992 the government consolidated VET schools to launch the Institute of Technical Education (ITE), intentionally positioning it as a post secondary institution with a distinct identity and place in the education system. The policy, with all the negative connotations about tracking by ability, met with initial skepticism and disdain. Against the odds, the ITE fulfilled its mandate of offering the least academically inclined 10th grade completers a viable pathway to the labor market. Today, it is recognized internationally as an authentic competency-based training system whose occupational standards for skills acquisition are developed in genuine partnership with industry. The ITE's acceptance by the public is the culmination of years of perseverance on multiple fronts: investment in world-class facilities, well-governed ties with industry, excellent institutional leadership and management, and public campaigns substantiated by acceptable employment outcomes for its graduates. The ITE's experience exemplifies the need for careful and sustained effort, through successive 5-year strategic planning exercises over the last 20 years, to ensure successful integration of VET into the education system.[13]

"Implementation is policy!" was how one senior policy maker described the importance attached by the government to implementation. In the education and training sector, the commitment to skills building—a cornerstone of Singapore's development strategy since the country's founding—starts at the top and is transmitted effectively down the line. It is understood that policy pronouncements will remain on paper unless accompanied by governance arrangements to motivate, engage, and empower leaders at all levels, including those in schools. The government places a heavy premium on the selection and training of school leaders, gives them the autonomy and budgets to develop distinctive programs to fulfil their own institution's mandate, and measures progress against agreed performance indicators. In this sense, the approach uses business practices to encourage implementation for results.

Learning from others is a hallmark of Singapore's own development experience. Ideas from Japan, Germany, and the United States, for example, initially informed the way the ITE approached the development of its own training curricula and pedagogy. Yet learning from others does not mean copying exactly what others have done; it invariably incorporates a high dose of learning by doing, often embarked upon without waiting for conditions to be ideal. Success with simple projects creates a virtuous loop for feedback and learning, generates confidence, and establishes a platform, or perhaps only a foothold, for the next phase, thereby setting off an upward spiral of learning by doing. Singapore insists on learning by doing because, frankly, it is the only effective way to build domestic capacity for conceptualizing policy reforms and sustaining successful implementation.

Notes

1. See http://www.undp.org/content/undp/en/home/sdgoverview/mdg_goals.html.

2. For details, see United Nations (2014).

3. For details on iCarnegie, see http://www.cmu.edu/news/stories/archives/2013/february/feb18_icarnegiemexico.html.

4. It is beyond the scope of this book to summarize the extensive literature on industrial policy. The discussion here is therefore limited to the authors' interpretation of recent trends in development policies and practices in emerging economies and related observations regarding skills and workforce development.

5. Details on the partnership between the City Colleges of Chicago and industry leaders may be found at http://www.ccc.edu/menu/Pages/Reinvention_F_Occupational.aspx; see also CCC 2013.

6. By 2001 nearly 40,000 students were enrolled in Regional Technical Colleges, up from less than 5,000 students in 1975 (Leigh-Doyle 2012).

7. CCC is the largest system of community colleges in Illinois. With seven geographically dispersed constituent colleges, it enrolls a total of 120,000 students. The insights on CCC discussed here come from a field visit to CCC in April 2013 by a World Bank team that included two of the authors of this study. Additional details about CCC and the Reinvention reform may be found at www.ccc.edu.

8. The amount includes operations in noneducation sectors, where the government counterpart for the World Bank operation is an agency other than the Ministry of Education. The share of funding channeled through entities other than the Ministry of Education has fluctuated between 25 percent and 47 percent during the 2000s. In FY 2009 the share was 52 percent of the International Development Association (IDA) credits and 48 percent of the International Bank for Reconstruction and Development (IBRD) loans. Standard components in VET operations include those that support competency-based curricula, skills testing, instructor development, institutional management, private sector engagement, labor market observatory, and management information systems.

9. Examples of recent operations entering the World Bank's portfolio with a strong focus on demand-driven VET investments include those in Bangladesh, China, Ghana, India, and Mozambique.

10. See Metzger *et al.* (2004) for an example of systematic learning among the leaders of five VET institutions in four countries. They formed a study group whose members took turns, over a period of nearly five years between February 1996 and December 2000, to host site visits to provide feedback and learn from each other.

11. See these and other results summarized in figure 5.15.

12. Organized under an agreement during 2006–09 between the World Bank and the government of Singapore, with support from the government of Norway, the study visits exemplify the type of sustained, programmatic cross-country exchange that the World Bank convenes to foster and inform dialogue for policy reform in its partner countries. The tripartite collaboration accomplished the following: (1) an integrated program of three visits over four years that benefited 115 African policy makers from 10 countries, 30 World Bank staff, and 30 guests, among them speakers and African journalists; (2) a high-level policy conference in Tunis, Tunisia, in 2009 attended by 44 African ministers of finance and of education from 27 countries and the West Bank and Gaza; and (3) four formal publications (Fredriksen 2010; Fredriksen and Tan 2008; Lee *et al.* 2008; and Yusuf and Nabeshima 2012). As Tan 2015 indicates, the longer term impacts are more difficult to quantify but clearly more consequential.

13. Law (2015) provides insights into how Singapore's Institute of Technical Education tackled many of its developmental challenges to become a recognized international leader in the field. Strengthening and consolidating technical centers originally set up

under the Economic Development Board in partnership with various foreign firms and countries is another important aspect of establishing VET as an integral, yet distinct, part of the education system. That process also took about 20 years, between 1972 and 1993 (Tan and Nam 2012).

References

ACET (African Center for Economic Transformation). 2014. *2014 African Transformation Report: Growth with Depth.* Accra: African Center for Economic Transformation. Accra, Ghana. Available at http://acetforafrica.org/publications/preview-of-the-african -transformation-report/.

ADB (Asian Development Bank). 2008. *Education and Skills: Strategies for Accelerated Development in Asia and the Pacific.* Manila: ADB.

———. 2009. *Good Practice in Technical and Vocational Education and Training.* Manila: ADB.

———. 2014. *Innovative Strategies in Technical and Vocational Education and Training for Accelerated Human Resource Development in South Asia.* Manila: ADB.

Aiginger, Karl. 2014. "Industrial Policy for a Sustainable Growth Path." Policy Paper 13, Welfare, Wealth and Work for Europe, Vienna, Austria.

Altenburg, Tilman. 2011. "Industrial Policy in Developing Countries: Overview and Lessons from Seven Country Cases." Discussion Paper 4/2011, Deutsches Institut für Entwicklungspolitik (German Development Institute), Bonn.

Ansu, Yaw, and Jee-Peng Tan. 2012. "Skills Development for Economic Growth in Sub-Saharan Africa: A Pragmatic Perspective." In *Good Growth and Governance in Africa: Rethinking Development Strategies,* edited by Akbar Noman, Kwesi Botchwey, Howard Stein, and Joseph E. Stiglitz, 462–497. Oxford: Oxford University Press.

Bailey, David, Helena Lenihan, and Josep-Maria Arauzo-Carod. 2011. "Industrial Policy after the Crisis." *Policy Studies* 32 (4): 303–08.

Benson, John, Howard Gospel, and Ying Zhu, eds. 2013. *Workforce Development and Skill Formation in Asia.* London: Routledge.

Block, Fred, and Matthew R. Keller. 2011. *State of Innovation: The U.S. Government's Role in Technology Development.* Boulder, CO: Paradigm Publishers.

CCC (City Colleges of Chicago). 2013. *5 Year Plan: Strategic Initiatives and Objectives, 2013–2018.* Chicago: City Colleges of Chicago. http://www.ccc.edu/Documents /city%20colleges%20of%20chicago_5-year%20plan_2013-2018.pdf.

Cimoli, Mario, Giovanni Dosi, and Joseph E. Stiglitz. 2009. "The Political Economy of Capabilities Accumulation: The Past and Future of Policies for Industrial Development." In *Industrial Policy and Development: The Political Economy of Capabilities Accumulation,* edited by Mario Cimoli, Giovanni Dosi, and Joseph E. Stiglitz, 1–18. Oxford: Oxford University Press.

Collins, Jim. 2005. *Good to Great and the Social Sectors: A Monograph to Accompany Good to Great.* New York: HarperCollins.

Devlin, Robert, and Graciela Moguillansky. 2013. "What's New in the Industrial Policy in Latin America?" In *The Industrial Policy Revolution,* edited by Justin Lin and Joseph Stiglitz, 276–317. New York: Palgrave Macmillan.

Dhéret, Claire, and Martina Morosi. 2014. "Towards a New Industrial Policy for Europe." EPC Issue Paper 78, European Policy Centre, Brussels.

Fernandez -Stark, Karina, Penny Bamber, and Gary Gereffi. 2011a. "The Fruit and Vegetable Global Value Chain: Economic Upgrading and Workforce Development." In *Skills for Upgrading: Workforce Development and Global Value Chains in Developing Countries*, edited by Gary Gereffi, Karina Fernandez-Stark, and Phil Psilos, 13–74. Durham, NC: Center on Globalization, Governance & Competitiveness, Duke University.

———. 2011b. "The Offshore Services Global Value Chain: Economic Upgrading and Workforce Development." In *Skills for Upgrading: Workforce Development and Global Value Chains in Developing Countries*, edited by Gary Gereffi, Karina Fernandez-Stark, and Phil Psilos, 132–89. Durham, NC: Center on Globalization, Governance & Competitiveness, Duke University.

Fredriksen, Birger. 2010. "Sustaining Educational and Economic Momentum in Africa." Working Paper 195, Africa Region, World Bank, Washington, DC.

Fredriksen, Birger, and Tan Jee-Peng, eds. 2008. *An African Exploration of the East Asian Education Experience*. Washington, DC: World Bank.

Gill, Indermit, Fred Fluitman, and Amit Dar, eds. 2000. *Vocational Education and Training Reform: Matching Skills to Markets and Budgets*. Joint Study of the World Bank and the International Labour Office. Washington, DC: World Bank.

Hausmann, Ricardo, and Bailey Klinger. 2006. "Structural Transformation and Patterns of Comparative Advantage in the Product Space." CID Working Paper 128, Center for International Development, Harvard University, Cambridge, MA.

———. 2007. "The Structure of the Product Space and the Evolution of Comparative Advantage." CID Working Paper 146, Center for International Development, Harvard University, Cambridge, MA.

Hidalgo, Cesar A., Bailey Klinger, Albert Lázló Barabási, and Ricardo Hausmann. 2007. "The Product Space Conditions the Development of Nations." *Science* 317 (5837): 482–85.

ILO (International Labour Office). 2008. "Skills for Improved Productivity, Employment Growth and Development." Report V, International Labour Conference, 97th Session. International Labour Office, Geneva.

———. 2010. *A Skilled Workforce for Strong, Sustainable and Balanced Growth: A G20 Training Strategy*. Geneva: International Labour Office.

Inter-Agency Working Group on TVET Indicators. 2012. *Proposed Indicators for Assessing Technical and Vocational Education and Training*. Turin, Italy: European Training Foundation; Geneva: ILO; Paris: UNESCO.

Lall, Sanjaya. 2000. "Skills, Competitiveness and Policy in Developing Countries." QEH Working Paper 46, Oxford Department of International Development, University of Oxford, Oxford.

Law, Song Seng. 2015. *A Breakthrough in Vocational and Technical Education: The Singapore Story*. Singapore: World Scientific Publishing.

Lee, Sing Kong, Goh Chor Boon, Birger Fredriksen, and Tan Jee-Peng, eds. 2008. *Toward a Better Future: Education and Training for Economic Development in Singapore since 1965*. Washington, DC: World Bank and National Institute of Education.

Leigh-Doyle, Sue. 2012. "Workforce Development: Ireland." SABER Multiyear Country Report 2012, World Bank, Washington, DC. http://wbgfiles.worldbank.org /documents/hdn/ed/saber/supporting_doc/CountryReports/WFD/SABER_WfD_ Ireland_Multiyear_CR_2012.pdf.

Lin, Justin Yifu, and Célestin Monga. 2012. "Growth Identification and Facilitation: The Role of the State in the Dynamics of Structural Change." In *New Structural Economics: A Framework for Rethinking Development and Policy*, edited by Justin Yifu Lin, 81–112. Washington, DC: World Bank.

Martinez-Fernandez, Cristina, and Kyungsoo Choi. 2013. "An Overview of Skills Development Pathways in Asia." In *Skills Development for Inclusive and Sustainable Growth in Developing Asia-Pacific*, edited by Robert Maclean, Shanti Jagannathan, and Jouko Sarvi, 13–40. Dordrecht, The Netherlands: Springer Science+Business Media B.V. for the Asian Development Bank.

Mazzoleni, Roberto, and Richard R. Nelson. 2009. "The Roles of Research at Universities and Public Labs in Economic Catch-Up." In *Industrial Policy and Development: The Political Economy of Capabilities Accumulation*, edited by Mario Cimoli, Giovanni Dosi, and Joseph E. Stiglitz, 378–408. Oxford: Oxford University Press.

Mazzucato, Mariana. 2011. *The Entrepreneurial State*. London: Demos.

Mehrota, Santosh. 2009. "The International Market for Public Policies on Skills Development: The Special Case of India." Paper prepared for the NORRAG Conference on Policy Transfer or Policy Learning: Interactions between International and National Skills Development Approaches for Policy Making, Geneva, June 25–26.

Metzger, Christopher, Hidenori Fujita, Seng Song Law, Robert Zemsky, Jean-Étienne Berset, and Marcus Iannozzi. 2004. "Vocational Training and Education." In *Learning through Collaborative Research*, edited by N. F. McGinn, 91–145. New York: Routledge Falmer.

MIGA (Multilateral Investment Guarantee Agency). 2006. *The Impact of Intel in Costa Rica: Nine Years after the Decision to Invest*. Washington, DC: World Bank Group/MIGA.

Noland, Marcus, and Howard Pack. 2002. "Industrial Policies and Growth: Lessons from International Experience." In *Economic Growth: Sources, Trends, and Cycles*, edited by Norman Loayza and Raimundo Soto, 251–308. Santiago: Central Bank of Chile.

NORRAG. 2013. "2012: The Year of Global Reports on TVET, Skills & Jobs—Consensus or Diversity?" *NORRAG News* 48 (Graduate Institute of International and Development Studies (IHEID), Geneva. http://www.norrag.org/fileadmin/Full%20 Versions/NN48.pdf.

Nübler, Irmgard. 2011. "Industrial Policies and Capabilities for Catching Up: Framework and Paradigms." Employment Sector Employment Working Paper 77, International Labour Office, Geneva.

O'Hare, Daniel. 2008. "Education in Ireland: Evolution of Economic and Education Policies since the Early 1990s." In *An African Exploration of the East Asian Education Experience*, edited by Birger Fredriksen and Tan Jee-Peng, 287–349. Washington, DC: World Bank.

Pack, Howard. 2011. "Industrial Policy in Historical Perspective." Paper presented at the American Economic Association 2011 Annual Meeting, Denver, January 7–9.

Pack, Howard, and Kamal Saggi. 2006. "The Case for Industrial Policy: A Critical Survey." *World Bank Research Observer* 21 (2): 267–95.

Padmini, H. A., A. Keshav Bharadway, and T. R. Gopalakrishnan Nair. 2009. "Approaches to Curriculum and Teaching Materials to Bring Out Better-Skilled Software Engineers—An Indian Perspective." In *Proceedings of the First International Conference on Education and New Learning Technologies*. Valencia: International Academy of Technology, Education and Development.

PASET (Partnership for Skills in Applied Science, Engineering and Technology). 2015. "Building Capacity in Scientific and Technical Fields for the Priority Sectors in Africa" (brochure). http://www.universityworldnews.com/article.php?story=201307181 62040419.

Philips, D. 1989. "Neither a Borrower nor a Lender Be? The Problems of Cross-National Attraction in Education." *Comparative Education* 25 (3): 267–74.

Psilos, Phil, and Gary Gereffi. 2011. "Workforce Development in the Global Economy: Linking Skills and Capabilities to Upgrading." In *Skills for Upgrading: Workforce Development and Global Value Chains in Developing Countries*, edited by Gary Gereffi, Karina Fernandez-Stark and Phil Psilos, 1–12. Durham, NC: Center on Globalization, Governance & Competitiveness, Duke University.

Raffe, D. 2011. "Cross-National Differences in Education-Work Transitions." In *The Oxford Handbook of Lifelong Learning*, edited by Manuel London, 312–28. New York: Oxford University Press.

Reinert, Erik S. 2010. "Developmentalism." Technology Governance and Economic Dynamics Working Paper 34, The Other Canon Foundation, Hvasser, Norway, and Tallinn University of Technology, Tallinn, Estonia.

Rodrik, Dani. 1999. *The New Global Economy and Developing Countries: Making Openness Work*. Washington, DC: Overseas Development Council.

———. 2008. "Industrial Policy: Don't Ask Why, Ask How." *Middle East Development Journal* 1 (1): 1–29.

———. 2014. "Green Industrial Policy." *Oxford Review of Economic Policy* 30 (3): 469–91.

Spar, Debora. 1998. "Attracting High Technology Investment: Intel's Costa Rican Plant." Foreign Investment Advisory Service Occasional Paper 11, International Finance Corporation and World Bank, Washington, DC.

Stiglitz, Joseph E., Justin Yifu Lin, and Célestin Mongga. 2013. "The Rejuvenation of Industrial Policy." Policy Research Working Paper 6628, World Bank, Washington, DC.

Sudan, Randeep. 2013. "Next Generation Operations: Mexico First: Mexico IT Industry Development Project." Presentation at the Education Staff Development Program (ESDP), Workforce Development Module, February 5, World Bank, Washington, D.C.

Tan, Jee-Peng. 2015. "Sharing Singapore's Achievements in Education with Africa." In *50 Years of Singapore and the United Nations*, edited by Tommy Koh, Li Lin Chang, and Joanna Koh. Singapore: World Scientific Publishing.

Tan, Jee-Peng, and Yoo-Jeung Joy Nam. 2012. "Pre-employment Technical and Vocational Education and Training: Fostering Relevance, Effectiveness and Efficiency." In *The Right Skills for the Job? Rethinking Training Policies for Workers*, edited by Rita Almeida, Jere Behrman, and David Robalino, 67–103. Washington, DC: World Bank.

United Nations. 2014. "Open Working Group Proposal for Sustainable Development Goals." http://www.un.org/ga/search/view_doc.asp?symbol=A/68/970.

Valerio, Alexandria, and Bernado Vasconcellos. 2011. "Skills Development and Training: Official Development Assistance." Unpublished. Human Development Network, World Bank, Washington, DC.

Wadhwa, Vivek, Una Kim de Vitton, and Gary Gereffi. 2008. *How the Disciple Became the Guru: Is it Time for the U.S. to Learn Workforce Development from Former Disciple India?* Durham, NC: Edmund T. Pratt Jr. School of Engineering, Duke University, and Harvard Law School, Harvard University, Cambridge, MA.

Weiss, John. 2005. "Export Growth and Industrial Policy: Lessons from the East Asian Miracle Experience." ADB Institute Discussion Paper 26, Asian Development Bank Institute, Tokyo.

World Bank. 1991. "Vocational and Technical Education and Training." World Bank Policy Paper. Washington, DC.

———. 2012a. *World Development Report 2013: Jobs.* Washington, DC: World Bank.

———. 2012b. *Youth Employment Programs: An Evaluation of World Bank and International Finance Corporation Support.* Washington, DC: Independent Evaluation Group, World Bank.

Yusuf, Shahid, and Kaoru Nabeshima. 2012. *Some Small Economies Do It Better: Rapid Growth and Its Causes in Singapore, Finland, and Ireland.* Washington, DC: World Bank.

Yusuf, Shahid, William Saint, and Kaoru Nabeshima. 2009. *Accelerating Catch-Up: Tertiary Education for Growth in Sub-Saharan Africa.* Washington, DC: World Bank.

Market and Government Roles in Workforce Development

In hypothetical perfect markets, the government would have a limited or indeed no role in skills development. Individuals would recoup, through higher earnings, their investment of money and time to acquire skills, and firms likewise would obtain their returns from investing in worker training through the increased productivity of their workforce. Yet practically no country in the world relies solely on market mechanisms to guide investments in skills development. Government action runs the gamut, from subsidizing training to providing services directly to setting standards and regulations for skills provision and skills certification, and so on. How should these actions be understood in relation to failures in the market for skills development? How can the public and private sectors complement each other more effectively in skills development?

Following a long tradition in the literature, market failures that impede skills investments may be grouped, for analytical purposes, under three main rubrics: labor market imperfections, capital market imperfections, and decision-making failures. A detailed explanation of the impact on skills investment can be found in Robalino, Almeida, and Behrman (2012). What follows below is a brief summary.

Labor market imperfections reduce the efficiency of training investments. When a firm incurs costs to train its workers, it expects productivity to rise and therefore to reap benefits that at least offset the cost of the training. But this expectation may not materialize if trained workers quit their jobs (too soon) for higher wages offered by other firms, typically those that did not invest in training. Poaching behavior dampens employers' incentives to train and fosters conditions for suboptimal levels of investment in skills (e.g., Brunello and De Paola 2004; Snower 2000; Wolf and Erdle 2009). Market imperfections may also take the form of information externalities that affect the behavior of training providers. Individuals and their employers may be interested in new skills, but training providers may not respond accordingly, particularly if the response entails heavy investment to create new course offerings. If the new offerings fail, the full cost of the failure would fall on the first movers among training providers. On the other hand, if the offerings prove successful, other providers might enter the market and reduce the pioneers' return on their investment. These sources of market imperfections identify areas for possible public policy, for example by encouraging the pooling of training funds across employers in a given industry or by subsidizing the costs of developing common course curricula in domains of high demand by industry.

It is important, however, to recognize the limitations of supply-led interventions to move countries out of a low-skills trap. In the absence of a strong and sustained demand for skills, an increase in the supply merely enables employers to fill their vacancies relatively easily, which shifts market power in their favor and allows them to drive down the wage premium of skilled workers relative to the unskilled. As the skills premium falls, individuals' incentive to acquire new skills also weakens (e.g., Brunello 2001; Snower 2000). Eventually, the economy slides back into a low-skills equilibrium and thwarts the hoped-for prospect of faster growth through an increase in skills supply.

Capital market imperfections shrink the financing options available to individuals who might benefit from acquiring more skills. Limited information about the creditworthiness of prospective trainees and uncertainty about the impact of training on productivity and earnings inevitably reduce the willingness of financial institutions to extend credit for skills training (Robalino and Almeida 2012; Snower 2000; Wolf and Erdle 2009). Lenders overcome these reservations by charging a high-risk premium on loans used for training purposes. In addition, because human capital can neither be used as collateral against loan default nor provide the basis for an equity investment, lenders are also likely to limit both the number and the size of such loans. Some potential borrowers will therefore be unable to finance their training, particularly for technical and vocational training where the diversity in training options, the lack of information about course quality and effectiveness, and the type of clientele drawn to such options all combine to increase the costs of due diligence for lenders. To relax capital market constraints, many governments, especially in wealthier countries, offer some form of subsidized financial aid to enable individuals to invest in skills acquisition. Examples are China, Chile, Finland, Thailand, and the United States.

Coordination and other decision-making failures can hurt job creation, economic growth, and employment. Such decision-making failures can trigger a vicious cycle that settles at a low-skills equilibrium. Firms shun innovations and the adoption of new technology because workers lack the relevant skills to make the investments worthwhile, and workers, for their part, take no steps to invest in upgrading their skills or learning new ones because there are no jobs requiring those skills (Aiyar 2003; Robalino and Almeida 2012; Robalino, Almeida, and Behrman 2012). Government efforts to break such vicious cycles also can fall victim to decision-making failures, such as the lack of coordination across government ministries. These issues may require the creation of purposeful structures, for example, India's National Skills Development Corporation, and mechanisms to foster informed, timely, and accountable decision making. More generally, underinvestment in skills may also stem from decisions by individuals and firms based on poor information and from the tendency, especially among young adults, to discount future earnings at far higher rates than might be socially optimal. The result is to reduce the returns that individuals expect from their skills investment and, by implication, their incentive to invest (Finegold 1991; Robalino and Almeida 2012).

Some decision-making failures can be prevented or attenuated in their adverse impact by improving the quality of information and making it more widely available. Examples include measures in countries such as Chile, Colombia, Italy, and the United States to inform young adults about training options, graduate skills, career paths, job prospects, and earnings profiles. Key features in these countries' initiatives include the following:

- Chile's Mi Futuro collects information from education institutions on graduate outcomes and pairs it with data from tax and pension administrations to make publicly available information on the incomes of graduates of professional and technical programs. This information provides an additional layer of transparency and accountability to the rapidly expanding tertiary education sector.[1]
- Colombia's Sistema Nacional de Información de Educación Superior (SNIES) and Observatorio Laboral para la Educacion (OLE) provide information to help families evaluate the quality and potential benefits of various courses of study. The SNIES, designed to be a comprehensive information system on higher education, provides information on programs and courses of study, socioeconomic information on current students and graduates, and information on institutional governance, infrastructure, and funding arrangements to allow for monitoring of the higher education system and allow stakeholders to easily access information on its makeup and content. The OLE provides information on graduate characteristics and outcomes to guide students, employers, and schools. This information is paired with surveys to measure graduate satisfaction and sectoral studies to determine the demand for labor.[2]
- Italy's private consortium AlmaLaurea provides employers with information on program curricula and aggregate information on graduate cohorts and university graduates' curriculum vitae (CVs) (AlmaLaurea–Interuniversity Consortium n.d.). It aims to reduce the costs faced by firms and individuals associated with screening applicants and opportunities.[3] There is evidence that this service reduces graduate unemployment and increases wages and self-reported job satisfaction (Bagues and Sylos Labini 2009).

- The United States's the O*Net Online portal offers information disaggregated by occupation on average remuneration, skills, and competencies needed, as well as the usual qualification of practitioners of each occupation. This information is integrated with projections on future demand for various occupations, allowing users to search for "hot occupations" that promise bright job prospects upon graduation from necessary education and training.[4]

To summarize, both markets and governments can and do fail in skills development. Unfettered markets can exacerbate social injustice (Stiglitz 2010) by reducing opportunities for skills investment, especially among the disadvantaged. Yet neither can the effects of government failure be ignored. Estimates for the United States, for example, suggest that the welfare loss may well surpass that of the market failures targeted for correction by government action (Winston 2006). Under the circumstances, a pragmatic approach to skills development seems appropriate, especially one that gives prominence to experimentation, learning, and adaption in the search for solutions that are both relevant and productive.

The standardized scores presented in figure A.1 are calculated by taking the difference between a score and the sample mean and dividing it by the standard error. The resulting standardized score allows comparison of a country's score for each dimension relative to variation in the quality of policies and institutions observed across sample countries. The thresholds for the four levels of development specified in the SABER-WfD (Systems Approach for Better Results-Workforce Development) methodology—Latent, Emerging, Established, and Advanced—have also been standardized, allowing for the cutoffs between levels to be determined by the underlying data in the sample. This serves as a check on the appropriateness of thresholds defined by the SABER-WfD methodology. Results are presented separately by dimension because standardizing the cut-off values for each level of development yields values that vary slightly by dimension. The line of best fit reflects projected standardized scores based on per capita income.

Presenting standardized results does not change the substantive conclusions laid out in chapter 4 (section "Pattern in Dimension-Level Scores across Countries"). As with the unstandardized scores, the pattern suggests that the quality of policies and institutions increases with gross domestic product (GDP) per capita, though there is greater variation in scores at lower levels of income. For example, several countries with GDP per capita below $2,000 score as well as some countries with more than four times the annual per capita income across all dimensions. At higher levels of income, the quality of policies and institutions is markedly better. The scores for several countries at the upper end of the income scale have standardized SABER-WfD scores that are greater than the sample mean by more than 2.5 times the sample standard error.

Figure A.1 Relationship between Standardized Scores and GDP Per Capita, by Dimension

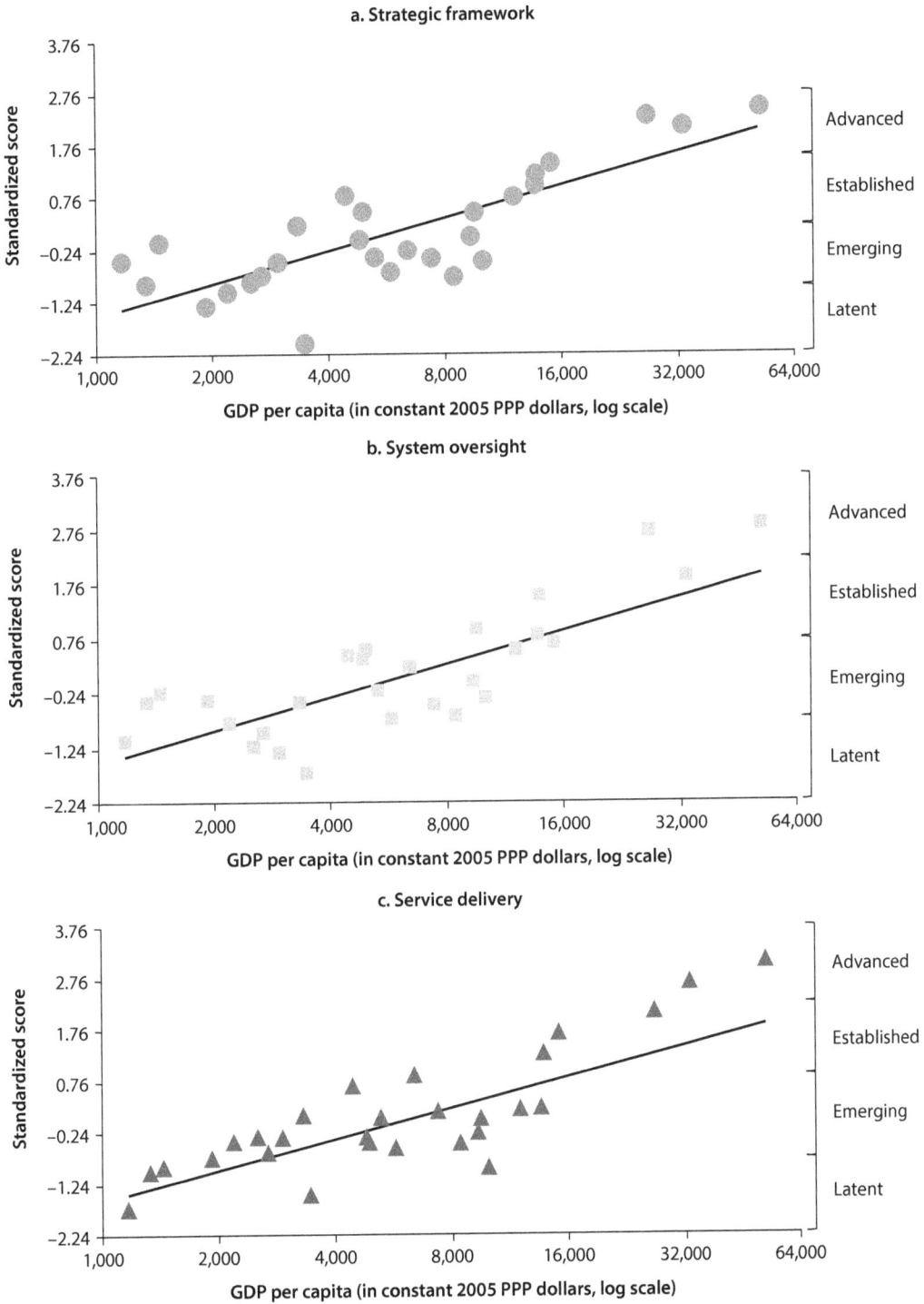

a. Strategic framework

b. System oversight

c. Service delivery

Source: World Bank calculation based on data for 27 countries and the West Bank and Gaza.
Note: Standardized scores refer to the difference between a score and the sample mean, divided by the standard error of the scores. GDP = gross domestic product; PPP = purchasing power parity.

Table A.1 Detailed Summary of the SABER-WfD Findings for 22 Countries

Findings by functional dimension	Policy goal	Findings by policy goal
Strategic framework: The sample countries find it more difficult to form and sustain strategic partnerships with employers than to articulate a direction for WfD or to ensure coordination of effort on specific priorities.	Direction	Countries do well at conceptualizing WfD strategy
		… but find it harder to mobilize high-level leaders to provide sustained public advocacy for it.
	Partnership	Countries generally do well at establishing an informed basis for stakeholder collaboration
		… but less well at forging effective and sustained engagement with employers for WfD.
	Coordination	Roles and responsibilities for WfD stakeholders are generally well-defined, especially in government.
		Effective implementation of strategic WfD initiatives at the leadership level is generally weak,
		… with evidence that clarity of roles must be backed by effective implementation of strategic initiatives.
System oversight: The sample countries have more difficulty with funding policy for VET than with assuring quality or creating pathways for skills acquisition	Funding policy	Efficiency of public funding for WfD receives more attention from policy makers than equity,
		… with CVET's efficiency receiving less attention than that of IVET or active labor market programs
		… and equity receiving rare attention across the board, even for programs intended for the poor.
		Private resources are being tapped for WfD in most countries.
	Quality assurance	On qualifications standards, formal frameworks are commonplace
		… but vary widely in robustness and scope of coverage.
		On skills certification, common certificates and testing for major occupations are trustworthy
		… but competency-based standards are often not yet system-wide.
		On accreditation, enforcing existing requirements is a common practice
		… more so than supporting service providers to meet standards for accreditation.
	Learning pathways	On preemployment VET, pathways for skills acquisition are generally well-defined and open
		… but public skepticism about VET remains and program articulation is weak.
		On continuing VET, most of the countries struggle with building a strong system
		… with recognition of prior learning being an area of special challenge.
		On programs for the disadvantaged, arrangements are diverse across countries
		… with many systems performing at the Established level.

table continues next page

Table A.1 Detailed Summary of the SABER-WfD Findings for 22 Countries (continued)

Findings by functional dimension	Policy goal	Findings by policy goal
Service delivery: A well-run system of training provision, one with public and private organizations accountable for and managed to achieve results in the job market, is rare among the sample countries.	Diversity and excellence	Vibrant training provision by nonstate institutions is commonplace
		… but countries tend to rely more on regulation than on incentives to drive quality.
		Public providers are generally not intentionally managed for excellence,
		… with rare use of institutional performance targets combined with institutional autonomy.
	Relevance of public programs	Provider-industry linkages are commonplace
		… but most arrangements are ad hoc and tend to focus on curriculum design.
		Provider-research links are rare
		… and are limited to the more economically developed countries.
		Staff quality receives modest attention
		… despite its relevance for public institutions' capacity to deliver industry relevant programs.
	System management	Data-driven system management is nascent
		… with providers in most countries required to report just administrative data
		… and few countries using in-depth analyses and routine feedback to learn and improve.

Source: World Bank construction based on data for 22 countries collected in the manner described in the book. The full sample contains 27 countries and the West Bank and Gaza, as follows: Armenia, Bulgaria, Chile, the Arab Republic of Egypt, Georgia, Grenada, Iraq, Ireland, Jordan, the Republic of Korea, the Lao People's Democratic Republic, the former Yugoslav Republic of Macedonia, Malaysia, Moldova, Morocco, Singapore, the Solomon Islands, Sri Lanka, St. Lucia, Tajikistan, Timor-Leste, Tunisia, Turkey, Uganda, Ukraine, Vietnam, and the Republic of Yemen. Excluded from this sample are six countries whose data came from an earlier prototype of the SABER-WfD data collection instrument; the arrangement and wording of items in that version of the instrument yielded, in the authors' judgment, data that were comparable to the rest of the sample mainly at the dimension level. These six countries are: Chile, Ireland, Korea, Singapore, Uganda, and Vietnam. Five countries had data for multiple years: Chile, Ireland, Korea, Malaysia, and Singapore.
Note: SABER = Systems Approach for Better Education Results; VET = Vocational Education and Training; IVET and CVET refer, respectively, to Initial VET and Continuing VET; WfD = workforce development.

Notes

1. For more information on Mi Futuro see: http://www.mifuturo.cl/.

2. For more information on SNIES see http://www.mineducacion.gov.co /sistemasdeinformacion/1735/w3-article-211868.html; and for more information on OLE see http://www.graduadoscolombia.edu.co/html/1732/w3-channel.html.

3. For more information AlmaLaurea see: http://www.almalaurea.it/sites/almalaurea.it /files/docs/info/almalaurea_morethan20years.pdf.

4. For more information on the O*Net program see: http://www.onetcenter.org /overview.html.

References

Aiyar, Shekhar. 2003. "The Human Capital Constraint: Of Increasing Returns, Educational Choice and Coordination Failure." *B.E. Journal of Macroeconomics* 3 (1): 1–26.

AlmaLaurea–Interuniversity Consortium. n.d. "AlmaLaurea since 1994: More than 20 Years of Activity." http://www.almalaurea.it/sites/almalaurea.it/files/docs/info/almalaurea_morethan20years.pdf.

Bagues, Manuel F., and Mauro Sylos Labini. 2009. "Do Online Labor Market Intermediaries Matter? The Impact of AlmaLaurea on the University-to-Work Transition." In *Studies of Labor Market Intermediation*, edited by David H. Autor, 127–54. Chicago: University of Chicago Press.

Brunello, Giorgio. 2001. "On the Complementarity between Education and Training in Europe." IZA Discussion Paper 309, Forschungsinstitut zur Zukunft der Arbeit (Institute for the Study of Labor), Bonn.

Brunello, Giorgio, and Maria De Paola. 2004. "Market Failures and the Under-Provision of Training." CESifo Working Paper 1286, Center for Economic Studies, Ludwig Maximilian University of Munich, Munich.

Finegold, David. 1991. "Institutional Incentives and Skill Creation: Preconditions for a High-Skill Equilibrium." In *International Comparisons of Vocational Education and Training for Intermediate Skills*, edited by Paul Ryan, 93–118. London: Falmer Press.

Robalino, David, and Rita Almeida. 2012. "Overview." In *The Right Skills for the Job? Rethinking Effective Training Policies for Workers*, edited by Rita Almeida, Jere Behrman, and David Robalino, 11–48. Washington, DC: Social Protection, Human Development Network, World Bank.

Robalino, David, Rita Almeida, and Jere Behrman. 2012. "Policy Framework: The Economic Rationale for Skills Development Policies." In *The Right Skills for the Job? Rethinking Effective Training Policies for Workers*, edited by Rita Almeida, Jere Behrman, and David Robalino, 49–66. Washington, DC: World Bank.

Snower, Dennis. 2000. "Creating Employment Incentives." In *Innovative Employment Initiatives*, edited by Bernd Marin, Daniele Meulders, and Dennis Snower, 317–46. Aldershot, UK: Ashgate.

Stiglitz, Joseph E. 2010. "Government Failure vs. Market Failure: Principles of Regulation." In *Government and Markets: Toward a New Theory of Regulation*, edited by Edward J. Balleisen and David A. Moss, 13–51. New York: Cambridge University Press.

Winston, Clifford. 2006. *Government Failure versus Market Failure: Microeconomics Policy Research and Government Performance.* Washington, DC: AEI-Brookings Joint Center for Regulatory Studies.

Wolf, Artjom, and Andrea Erdle. 2009. *Key Aspects of the Economics of Technical and Vocational Education and Training (TVET): Lessons Learned and Gaps to Be Filled.* Eschborn: Deutsche Gesellschaft für Technische Zusammenarbeit (GTZ).

Environmental Benefits Statement

The World Bank Group is committed to reducing its environmental footprint. In support of this commitment, the Publishing and Knowledge Division leverages electronic publishing options and print-on-demand technology, which is located in regional hubs worldwide. Together, these initiatives enable print runs to be lowered and shipping distances decreased, resulting in reduced paper consumption, chemical use, greenhouse gas emissions, and waste.

The Publishing and Knowledge Division follows the recommended standards for paper use set by the Green Press Initiative. The majority of our books are printed on Forest Stewardship Council (FSC)–certified paper, with nearly all containing 50–100 percent recycled content. The recycled fiber in our book paper is either unbleached or bleached using totally chlorine-free (TCF), processed chlorine-free (PCF), or enhanced elemental chlorine-free (EECF) processes.

More information about the Bank's environmental philosophy can be found at http://www.worldbank.org/corporateresponsibility.

green
press
INITIATIVE

www.ingramcontent.com/pod-product-compliance
Lightning Source LLC
Chambersburg PA
CBHW080426270326
41929CB00018B/3184